SUBURGATORY

SUBURGATORY

Twisted Tales from Darkest Suburbia

LINDA ERIN KEENAN

Guilford, Connecticut
An imprint of Globe Pequot Press

To buy books in quantity for corporate use
or incentives, call **(800) 962-0973**
or e-mail **premiums@GlobePequot.com**.

skirt! is an imprint of Globe Pequot Press.

Text design: Sheryl P. Kober
Editor: Lara Asher
Project editor: Meredith Dias
Layout: Joanna Beyer

Library of Congress Cataloging-in-Publication Data is available on file.

ISBN 978-0-7627-8019-8

Printed in the United States of America

10 9 8 7 6 5 4 3 2 1

This book is dedicated to the best man I could have ever chosen to have a son with, Steve Mendes, and the now boy-man who made life in Suburgatory a daily joy amid the madness, Frank Keenan Mendes. Also to my late Daddy, Joe Keenan, and my beloved, irreplaceable Mommy, Marie Thibodeau Keenan. If only you were here to see this all, Mommy.

Introduction

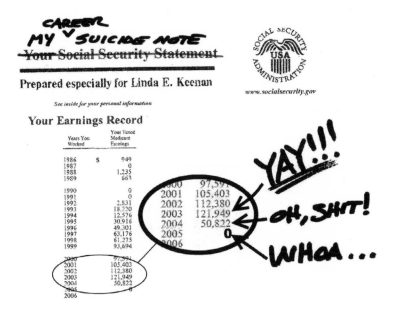

Behold, in graphic detail, the career suicide note of one Linda Erin Keenan. Each year since having my son and having the luxury to stay home with him, the Social Security Administration has quite graciously let me know, with this, my lifetime earnings statement, that after a decade of steady raises at work, I have gone from Hero in 2003, to pregnant and disabled with severe nausea in 2004, to Big Fat Zero in 2005 and beyond. Well, I prefer the term, "Unpaid Mommy, Raising America's Future," you woman-hating bureaucrats!

Every year when I find this hateful scrap of paper in the mailbox, I once again see the clearest evidence I have of how I tumbled so hard and fast from a trash-talking, urban CNN news writer in New York City to an unemployed, depressed, suddenly suburban, and *still* trash-talking stay-at-home mom. I do have an unstoppable potty mouth as you'll see in this book, and I'm not talking about diaper chat here.

This Career Suicide Social Security Earnings document, in a way, was my ticket into an utterly foreign place I now call *Suburgatory*, where potty mouths (and minds) like mine are about as rare as black people—in the 1 percent range, I'd say. Actually there are probably more black people than potty mouths, now that I think about it. In this strange land, I had a new baby, no friends, and not much more than a prescription for Zoloft to keep myself afloat. Apparently, the ticket was one-way, because I'm sure as hell still stuck in Suburgatory.

The original proposal for this book was picked by Warner Brothers in 2010, and you can see their imagining of Suburgatory on the ABC show of the same title, which debuted in Fall 2011. But while the TV series focuses on a transplanted teen from New York City, my book offers a vision of suburbia and contemporary American life that I witnessed when I myself was transplanted from the city after having my son. It is satirical local news that skewers mostly upper-middle-class American pieties and parenting obsessions (not least, my own). I also target racism, sexism, mommy wars, body self-hatred, sublimated suburban sexuality, and class warfare; willful ignorance to the broader world along with an America in decline; and the all-around bad behavior that I have seen raging underneath the surface of those obsessively tended suburban lawns and bikini lines.

Do those "isms" make this sound like that annoying late 1980s sociology class you skipped, or worse, *a women's studies course?!* Well, fear not, there's lots of swear words and dirty talk all over *Suburgatory*. (See later, my combination of both obsessions with the lawns and the bikini lines, in my fake ad for *Suburgatory*'s new, hot landscaping service: "The Lawnzilian.")

Tessa, the teenage character created by ABC's *Suburgatory*, was forced by the man in her life—her dad—to leave her beloved city life for this supposed suburban utopia, which the show creator says was inspired by her own experience as a teen. As I wrote about in my book proposal, I followed the same trajectory—with my husband, Steve. Steve couldn't imagine raising our son in New York, which had become too unimaginably scary to him once he gazed upon his new, miraculous baby boy clone. I did not feel this way. But I couldn't imagine handling my scary-intense job and being a mom at the same time. (Several mom friends *could* handle it—though not most—it must be said. Sorry, bra-burning, second-wave feminists disgusted with their weak, pathetic daughters! You can ask my weary shrink and pharmaceutical-battered liver: I simply couldn't cut it.)

OK, here's the point where you might be thinking of flinging your book or iPad or Kindle across the room, and saying to yourself: *Oh my God, I've bought another whiny white mommy book. What was I thinking? Here she goes, complain, complain, annoying, spoiled whiny white mommy. I'm toning her!* Well, let me explain precisely what this whiny white mommy is complaining about.

I fully acknowledge that I am among the luckiest of women in the luckiest place anywhere on the planet. I *chose* to stay at home and that's not a choice most can make. That Big Fat Zero on my Career Suicide Note did not bankrupt me. I made good money for a handful of years, and have a husband with a good salary, and we are also both pathologically cheap.

How cheap are we? So cheap that we could swing living in modest homes in expensive suburbs with great schools. But full disclosure: This luxury was subsidized by money I inherited when both my parents died (by the time I turned twenty-nine). Considering their modest salaries as teacher and career guidance expert in my hometown of Albany, New York (black/hispanic population near 40 percent—take *that*, whitey-town suburbia!), the fact that they amassed any savings at all after sending three daughters to pricey colleges amazes me. Clearly they were cheap, too—or, to use my technical term, "Super Crazy Mega Cheap."

My problem, and of course it is a problem *only* in the upper-middle-class sense of the word, is that abruptly leaving my career for suburban mommyhood made me a foreigner in a place where conformity was king, subversion seemed policed, and where I often felt like I had been taken hostage by an adult Girl Scout troop.

No surprise that my first friends in suburbia were *actual foreigners*. Naoko and Yuki were my treasured Japanese lady friends who fit in far better than I did, even though they weren't part of the rich "Power Asian" set, a significant demographic in my new land. "Rinda, this my home now!" Naoko would say, with several kids to take care of and a husband deployed in Iraq (and now, *sigh*, he's in Afghanistan. *Semper Fi*, Kevin Conway.) Still, she somehow found time to scrapbook, and, oh, work overnights at a place where she championed and cared for the severely disabled. What she lacked in language skills, she more than made up for with her indomitable spirit and trays of homemade sushi rolls. I wasn't the least bit surprised at the strength we all saw after the Japanese earthquake. Not me, not after Naoko and Yuki, who's a gorgeous beam of steel herself.

But what made *me* a foreigner? Really, it was my love of the transgressive and the unspeakable, spoken out loud. I've always been this way. As a seven-year-old in 1977, I drove my very conservative, Depression-era mother insane after I read the book *William's Doll* and began my own tiny fag hag crusade on behalf of "sissies" everywhere.

No surprise, I was the all-purpose outcast of my Catholic school—St. Bully's of the All Sadists—where my only outlet from constant harassment was to furtively read Judy Blume's *Deenie* (the one where Deenie touches her "special place" with a washcloth! God, I'm still aroused thirty years later).

No surprise that my sole childhood friend was the only Jew my Irish Catholic family really knew—Sheryl Olinsky—who set me up for a lifetime of Heeb-lovin' and Chinese-food eatin', and whose Barry Manilow and purple-powered Bat Mitzvah was the defining social event of my childhood. Pretty much the only social event, now that I think about it.

And no surprise I ended up in New York, a glorious Jew-zapalooza and Homo Heaven rolled into one, working in a place where having an eye for the deranged and twisted was not just tolerated, but a job requirement. For me, my truest home was a network TV newsroom.

Earnest moments are rare for me, and here comes one of them: I felt genuinely grateful, especially after 9/11 at CNN, that in my own tiny deskbound way, writing hermit-like on my bits of anchor copy, I got to call bullshit on asshole thugs on a global scale, on a daily basis. "Oh, I see, crazy Taliban nut-jobs, you plan to tip over a brick wall on top of an 'accused homosexual?' Now you're stoning a thirteen-year-old who was raped because she 'asked for it'? Allow me to help tell the world how sick and horrible you are!"

And beyond that ample satisfaction, I had the social benefits. I had found a family of trash-talkers like me, and we all relished incidents of guests gone wild. To get a control room full of satellite jockeys, camera guys, and nail-gnawing producers to laugh, you need to bring it hard, like the night when one guest, comedian Bill Maher, discussed basketball player Kobe Bryant "trying to get some stanky on his hangdown. Oh, can you say that on CNN?" Anchor Aaron Brown smoothly said, "I didn't understand most of those words," and for a few seconds neither did we as we speed-translated in our heads what the "hang-down" and "skanky" were. (For you nice, innocent types, "getting stanky on your hangdown" means getting a girl to have sex with you, as in "Linda was over last night? Did you get some stanky on your hangdown?") Once those seconds were up, we began bellowing at the fact that Maher had slipped that tender bit of sweet talk onto CNN air, with no apparent FCC fine either.

Another favorite was no-holds-barred sex columnist Dan Savage. When we booked him as a guest, I remember thinking in the back of my mind, *This guy could go X-rated, nasty-nuclear on live air.* He was picked to appear after a U.N. weapons inspector and Marine was reported as being an open and active member of the sadomasochistic "community." In the span of, um, four minutes? Savage hit the following topics: S&M ("sort of cops and robbers for grown-ups with your pants off, and it usually ends in masturbation"), vaginal and anal intercourse, balloon fetishes, smoking fetishes, and plushophiles (folks turned on by stuffed animals, and/or who dress up like stuffed animals. Savage's advice: "I hope there's a lot of Scotchguarded fabric on it."). He closed the interview by saying "Personally, I haven't spanked a Marine, but

I would make an exception for this man if I could see him first."

No one went ballistic about Maher's "stanky hang-down," but I think Savage's bravura performance almost got a few of us fired.

There were also moments of sublime retribution: When we, the lowly staff, saw our own private Ron Burgundys—the most imperious of anchors—humbled. Some were famous, or, more annoying still, wannabe famous. These are things that never ended up on Page Six in the *New York Post*, but damn well should have. (I should add that I have worked with or around dozens of anchors and reporters at three different news organizations. Good luck trying to figure out who I'm talking about. To tease you further on this, see the "Toddler or Anchor" piece later in the book, satire that's actually all true. And to the many nice, normal anchors or reporters? Know that your staff worships you for your sanity.)

A favorite was when one particularly annoying gasbag anchor left his wallet in the bathroom. Inside was a topless photo of his socially prominent, flat-chested girlfriend. (Is there any socially prominent woman who *isn't* flat-chested? And what about the booty? No booty either? Is there any preppy person with a booty?) That image got photocopied, by the way. Lucky for them this was back in the day, well before bare, semifamous A-cup titties would go viral within minutes. In any case, Sorry socially prominent, flat-chested, booty-free girlfriend. That's what you get for dating a pompous ass who can be nasty to his staff. A bumbling pompous ass who loses his wallet. He's booty-free too, by the way.

And there are few things sweeter than seeing the anchor who just humiliated your beloved work friend having his bald spot spray-covered with Hair-In-A-Can after the previous application of "hair" melted off in the rain. Or hearing a know-it-all anchor mispronounce a word everyone with a pulse should know, leaving the tech guys busting a rib laughing.

So the humor was on the jagged edge and the pace was intense. There were a handful of times when I was writing copy for Anderson Cooper about forty seconds before it was to come out of his mouth. Lucky for me Anderson can edit on the fly, on air, while these never-before-seen words popped from my fingers onto the prompter.

One time with Anderson, I blasted in, with literally seconds to spare, something thoughtlessly inappropriate about kidnapping victim Elizabeth Smart, in some misguided attempt to be "edgy." I watched Anderson process the words live and reject them, forcing him to vamp and instantaneously come up with something new and tasteful. Forced anchor vamping = massive fuckup for any copywriter. Crashing that hard, as we call it in news, left my hands sweating and my heart racing in one of the control rooms nicknamed the "Screamatorium."

By 2003 (the peak "Hero" moment on my Career Suicide Note), it was in my head that my life needed radical change. The seed had been planted two years before on 9/11. I heard the first plane crash from my apartment, just like millions of other New Yorkers, while Steve watched it fly in overhead. We were *by no means* affected in a truly personal way by 9/11, that is, having a direct family member or friend murdered that day, as so many other friends actually did. (Yeah, you heard me, murdered. I'm one of those liberal pukes who felt zero ambivalence shouting out "Fuck,

YEAH"—and then crying—when Bin Laden got it. Might have been a small fist pump, too. "About fucking time" is how this liberal reacted.)

But despite not having a family member or friend murdered, 9/11 had a cumulative effect on me: watching people cry in the streets holding "Missing" signs; seeing half my local firehouse wiped out; waking up to the smell of burning rubble for months after; being evacuated after a bomb threat with my boss screaming, "Everyone Get Out Now!"; writing endless stories about it at work; watching field producers come back from Ground Zero looking stricken; having guys in puffy hazmat suits walk around the office while my only protection from possible anthrax was an old, ugly Ann Taylor outfit. It added up, as I'm sure it did with countless other New Yorkers.

I vowed—quite uncharacteristically for a cynical sort like me—to take a chance on life, clean up my act, and have a baby. Steve said, "Sure, what the hell." I think 9/11 affected him too, though in a different way. His foul-mouthed daddy lion voice spoke to him saying, "There's no fucking way I'm raising my kid in this crime-ridden terror trap. *Roar!*" Not that we even had to debate the question. I knew I couldn't be a mom, keep my sanity, and continue in the Screamatorium; and we couldn't afford to stay in Manhattan on one salary. So off we went to the first of three suburbs over the next four years.

Within months of shvitzing in the Screamatorium, I found myself marooned in suburbia. Now, years later, with a happy son; a small house overrun with his brothers from different mothers; a select group of trash-talking friends; and Zoloft pills a-poppin', I see it as the birthplace of my new life as a thirty-something mom. I have a new set of satisfactions and, of course, a bigger ass. But at first suburbia seemed like nothing more than the graveyard for my twenty-something dreams. (*Sooo overdramatic, spoiled whiny white mommy! Trying to score the Pulitzer Prize for Overwriting? Good effort!*)

I had gone from 80 miles an hour to zero, and I had vastly underestimated the crash this staggering deceleration might cause. My landscape now included Wal-Mart on one end of the class scale and Whole Foods on the other; and crossover between the two looked nonexistent. Nearly everyone was white (*see* Whole Foods), except nannies, cleaning ladies, and yard workers (*see* Wal-Mart), and all the dads and the working moms I never met vanished on the 6:04 a.m. train.

Suburbanites seemed to me to have one-track minds, and mighty clean ones, too. They were about one business, and one business alone: baby and then child-raising. On paper, I didn't look so different from the other stay-at-home moms. They were mostly former professionals, too, some from Wall Street trading floors, which are easily as rough and tumble as any newsroom. But whatever edge these type-A women might have had now seemed gone, replaced by a version of hyper-vigilant parenting that was, to me, brutally boring and faintly absurd. They blathered on and on about how people without kids "just didn't get it." They seemed busy busy busy and, most important to me, appeared very short on laughs. One day I spotted some obscene playground graffiti and I was the only one even willing to acknowledge it, as in, "Look, that slide says VAGINA on it!" I wished I could share my glee with my potty-mouth ex-coworkers, since my new "coworker" moms had no interest. But they were back in the newsroom slamming a show together, while I was soon to establish myself as that weirdo mommy at Gymboree.

I knew very quickly that moving to the suburbs was a mistake when I realized that I missed my New York City doorman I'll call Rob, who was such a cliché of the portly, klutzy, up-in-your-business doorman that no self-respecting comedy writer would ever dream him up. (And in fact, one of the world's most successful comedy writers lived in my building as he, too, became a parent and eventually left for the suburbs: Adam McKay. How do I know this, since I've never met Adam McKay? Because Rob told me all about him, what a great guy he was, his nice wife and his adorable baby and his latest fantastic SNL sketch and. . . .)

Even at 11:30 p.m.—no, *especially* at 11:30 p.m.—when I was coming home to the East Village from work at CNN, exhausted, Rob would start in on an obscure Civil War fact, or deliver the results of the game he listened to on his hand-held radio, or describe the latest outing he had with girl-friend "Gladys" (her real name, like Gladys, is straight out of an old-school sitcom, just like Rob himself). Rob could and would talk about anything, and he would still be talking as the elevator doors closed. Years later, he's surely still talking. If Rob had suddenly found himself in my suburb, an army of concerned mommies would have dragged his fifty-year-old ass in for a special-ed evaluation, because Rob might well have had Asperger's.

So it was while pushing a baby stroller through a suburban mall (my new "town square") that I started missing not just my urban friends and job, but especially Rob, my go-to conversation machine, and all the other random faces I would bump into, sometimes literally, going about my city life. I had gone from living vertically with dozens of couples or single people in the same building (using the same elevators, clogging the same trash room), to living horizontally, families cut off from other families in their own cocoons: self-imposed segregation in a most concrete way. Feeling so cut off surely magnified a nasty case of postpartum depression and the crushing loneliness that came with it. That's when I turned into, well, the stay-at-home-mommy version of Rob.

I began talking to everyone, anywhere, anytime, all the time. Were people's facial cues telling me to back the fuck off, you crazy mommy? I didn't care. I followed a circuit of library story times with the devotion of a Dead Head (story time for tiny infants, mind you, who still don't know the difference between you and their own hand). I ate at the same diner every morning, ordering the same two-dollar egg sandwich until the waitress busting her ass recognized me. Yeah, she recognized me alright, as the spoiled mommy bitch who didn't have to work and wouldn't stop smiling at her, attempting pleasantries. I became an avid student of nanny culture and racially profiled them to find the most talkative ones. My inappropriate, sweeping generalization is that Caribbean nannies seemed the chattiest, and often cattiest, and therefore most desirable to me. I swear one favorite nanny showed such contempt for the parents of the boy-prince she was caring for that I thought her eyes were going to roll out and drop on to the park bench.

I attended a ragtag sing-along at a bookstore that usually attracted just a few passersby and me, the sad-sack regular with her quarrelsome baby. The sing-along leader was Jean, a sixty-something sweetheart, who was so scattershot I thought she was either drunk or mis-medicated. She would sort of punt on her kiddie playlist after just a few highly awkward songs and one day even said, "Linda, you take over."

She seemed more unhinged than me, and that's saying a lot. (Jean didn't have a car, I learned, when I saw her blowing around in the rain waiting for a bus on a hugely busy, dispiriting commercial thoroughfare. I picked her up. A suburbanite without a car: the ultimate outcast.)

And, as I mentioned, I joined a Gymboree class. That's where I met Bridget, Luv, as I called her in my head. Bridget, Luv, of course, was Irish; an older woman and a local legend among the baby-raising set for her savant-like knowledge of newborns. In my haze of postpartum depression, I had five of the worst seconds of my life in her class, when I actually forgot my beloved son's name, Frank. After class, I was so distraught I didn't want to leave Gymboree or Bridget, Luv, who said to me, "You have the bad baby blues, luv. I seen it a-tousand times."

All my pent-up loneliness plus my suppressed impropriety had to go somewhere, and that somewhere was online. Google my name and in a few clickety-clicks you'll find a sorry list of intimate grotesqueries I cataloged about myself with abandon when the meds finally kicked in, I got my writing act together, and I started submitting to the *Boston Globe* and the *Huffington Post*. I was determined to entertain myself, even if it meant looking like a self-obsessed exhibitionist begging for laughs.

Much of the indignity happened on Facebook, which is just vastly more diverse than my real life in suburbia. (Please friend me, Linda Erin Keenan, on Facebook if you're so inclined. The crazier you are, the better. I genuinely love it.) Like other lonely souls out there, I fell into that vortex of making Facebook my real, not-real community. How could snow-white suburbia compete with this picture? I realized it could be my own massively Awkward Facebook Family Photo: the homeless artist, the Pakistani mariner, the military fetishist, the Renaissance faire–loving transsexual lesbian massage therapist, the evangelical Republicans, my fashionista Mormon, the very sweet Sikh, the homeschooling pagan, two home-birthing doulas, the Texas BBQ restaurateur who promotes "burnt end sandwiches" right next to the hard-core vegan telling us that, say, my beloved Hot Pockets are killing me. All there and much much more in my wonderful Facebook nuthouse. Oh, and Buddy the Elf. He's there, too. He works for Santa. Says he's a real bastard.

In private, I pushed my boundaries further and began writing fake news satire, because eventually I went from bored to fascinated with the habits and fixations of upper-middle-class suburban life and parenting culture—like the bubble-wrapping of the affluent child—and what that says about America. Why do so many of the world's luckiest people seem so damn anxious?

I'm fascinated by the way some women mercilessly judge other women's choices, and what motivates the harshest proponents of the "pure" and "natural," especially in terms of breast-feeding. I see a lot of gory, competitive masochism in this area, like, say, "My nipples bled more than your nipples." "No, MY nipples bled more AND I got mastitis and then septic-shock!" Well, at the risk of having frozen bags of breast milk pelted at my door, I really don't get why people are so passionately interested in how I feed my child or how I use or view my own breasts. As I recall, they are *my* breasts, and that baby is *my* baby, and it's actually quite an intimate act to press on others with such vigor. I *also* don't understand the many women *and men* who vocally trash those who breast-feed their kids publicly, or for years and years. *None of your business.*)

I do have friends who believe strongly in breast-feeding, but they are *lovely*, advocate for *all* women, including the poor here and around the world, where breast-feeding can be a life-and-death choice for a baby if water is dirty. These activists are not toxically judgmental like, say, the "Breast-feeding Nazi Really a Nazi" I write about in the book. But vicious invective from others can be found all over the Internet. And passive-aggressive, thoughtless comments on breast-feeding, C-sections, epidurals, circumcision, staying at home versus working, and organic-food eating can have ugly impacts on fragile moms who choose to do things differently, or who might not even have a choice. It sure did on me, and on innumerable other friends.

Sadly, I think some of these movements inadvertently add to the yawning divide between rich and poor, or educated versus less educated. Not because the underlying goals of breast-feeding or eating organic food are unworthy, but because we are simply not set up in this country for subsidizing healthy food or fully supporting working mothers who breast-feed, poor or otherwise. Really, how does a woman working at low pay afford a souped-up Medela breast pump? How many women have jobs that will allow time to pump? Breast-feeding is only free if you don't put value on a woman's time.

Michelle Obama can exercise her ass off all over the country (and God love her for it), but until we end, say, distorting food industry subsidies, the poor and middle class have every incentive imaginable to eat cheap crap, and many of the "well meaning" make the less fortunate feel guilty about it. Eating like a locovore is all good and great, but it's often expensive, time-consuming, and simply impossible for people of average means.

So the poor and middle class seem to be getting less and less healthy, while affluent suburbia (and "urbia," too, for that matter) plies itself with every high-priced age-defying product, time-consuming betterment program or Whole Foods supplement, and basically jogs itself straight into its hale and hearty future. These days, Fat = Poor = Shame, as seen in "Woman Shops at Wal-Mart to Feel 'Pretty, Thin,'" among other pieces. Class, race, and religious collisions in mostly monochrome suburbia really interest me.

In a broader way, I also began thinking about America's diminished place in the world and how it might translate to the everyday business of raising a family; this whole idea of "living the dream" and maintaining a kind of phantom afflu-ence in the so-called Great Recession.

For instance, why did Amy Chua's tough-parenting *Tiger Mom* book strike such a chord? Do we fear she may be right, that we Americans are coddling our kids into medioc-rity? I wrote "Indian Child Taunted as 'New Jew' at Middle School" several years ago and thought Chua's "shaming" as an overdemanding mommy-shrew was quite similar to what happens to my overperforming immigrant Chaudry family.

Amidst this anxiety, I feel like in wealthy suburbia we not only Bubble-Wrap our kids from the broader world, but also ourselves, even as wars are being fought in our name by our less fortunate, rural, urban, and not comfortably suburban countrymen.

Meanwhile, I have seen the insistent creep of anti-Muslim, anti-"other," anti-teacher, and anti-union resentment that has been percolating since 9/11, but really seemed to explode as the economy collapsed and when President Obama was elected.

I was actually asked if I would prefer another doctor because the one I selected, a Sikh, wore a turban. You'll see that story, a Sikh gyno's desperate bid to keep patients, in an op-ed titled "I Am Certified Not Muslim . . . And I Love Your Feminine Area!" I labeled these op-eds **Shout Outs.**

On a more personal level, I'm interested in the way we transmit our biases and neuroses (especially my own), like female body self-hatred, to our kids. If you see pieces attacking women, just know that, very often, I am attacking myself. Not to be hopelessly cliché, but I love how a child's unspoiled view of the world challenges our own jaded beliefs and often leaves us flummoxed. If I used to call bullshit on the Taliban, my own son now calls bullshit on *me*; and if you're a parent, you surely get what I'm talking about. And I see the way we rewrite our sometimes sketchy pasts once we get to suburbia, because *You're a parent now, and that old life is over—especially the dirty, sexy parts.* I am fascinated and frankly sad that Suburgatory seems to be where sex goes to die, or at least gets suppressed. Well, it comes pouring out in this book, so get your raincoat!

I have also included history's worst advice columnist— **Dr. Drama**—who gets earnest questions and wants nothing more than to stir the shit out of your already messed-up life. This was inspired by the often riotous and toxic comment sections of real website advice columns, where anonymity lets people project and splay their crazy any which way.

And it should go without saying that anything labeled **Paid Advertising Content** is not a real ad. Believe me, I wish those were real. That would mean more money for me and my amazing agent, editors, and publisher. Also, as I mentioned above, I have lived in three suburbs in two states and have gotten ideas and themes from friends who live in a dozen more, mostly white, mostly affluent suburbs.

Suburgatory is *not* the town where I live now. I wouldn't stay here if it was, because some of the fictitious people you're about to meet are truly awful—and, hopefully, awfully hilarious. Any of the *real people* mentioned are, of course, used *solely* for parody purposes; Cynthia Nixon, a great actress and public school advocate, did *not* suddenly move to suburbia with her partner. Blogger Perez Hilton did *not* take a job as suburbia's zaniest new "Manny." *New York Times* columnist Tom Friedman did *not* threaten an all-powerful high-school guidance counselor with a nasty column. And surely, Wolf Blitzer did not really report "Live from the Lactation Room," though I'd give my left nut to see that actually happen for real. It's all satire and I'd hope Wolf, an anchor I long admired from afar at CNN, would get the joke.

So do I think of myself as a Big Fat Zero, like the Social Security Administration thinks I am, a no-paycheck parasite? No, because I neglected to mention that the Big Fat Zero did include a Plus One, and that would be the love of my life, my son, Frank Keenan Mendes. I only hope he never reads this book and realizes how sick and twisted his "Best Mom Ever" really is. Maybe after my funeral! And so I begin with a piece that's in large part true (though not the baptism part) about the near-year I spent as a secret atheist surrounded by simply wonderful Baptist believers. It is no exaggeration to say that these ladies helped save me from the abyss of postpartum depression. But sadly for them, they did not save me from hell.

Atheist Mom So Lonely
She Accepts Christ

Suburgatory, USA—Overwhelmed by the isolation of being a newly suburban stay-at-home mom in a town "not cool enough" for her, a local atheist has accepted Christ so she has someone to talk to.

Nonbeliever Mara Scully says her path to Christ was paved by the relentlessly friendly Baptists she met at Redemption Hill Church soon after moving here from Manhattan's East Village with her young son and husband. "They were so friendly and cool in a really weirdo kind of way and not at all like those plastic mommy-drones in my neighborhood. And I was so lonely. When I heard there were other moms all gathered in one place, I didn't care if it was a Baptist church or a crack house. The crack house would have been edgier and more my speed, but, you know, whatever."

Scully enjoyed the weekly church play zone, despite what she described as "a lot of crazy Christ stuff on the walls." She stresses that she is open-minded. "Just because I'm an atheist doesn't mean I'm bigoted. Is bigoted the right word?" It was nothing like what Scully recalled from her Catholic girlhood. "No 'scary Jesus,' no gory wounds at all! Their Jesus is sooo happy, and you know what? So are they!"

"They" are the members of Redemption Hill, who are puzzled by their new recruit. "She's not very pretty or turned out or 'New York,' is she?" whispered Pastor Kevin Barnett's wife, Karen. "And we've tried every polite way we can think of to tell her to stop swearing. Can you tell her?"

After attending the church twice weekly, enjoying potluck dishes like Tater Tot Pie, and developing warm if casual friendships, Scully said there were some contradictory feelings. "Sure, I find their views on abortion, gay rights, and a woman's place in the home repugnant and all. But after a while they began talking more and more about living a Godly life and I knew where the train was going. What was I going to do? Lose my only friends out here in the middle of Bumblefuck Nowheresville?"

Scully said she met with the pastor, talked about the Glory Christ can bring to a young family, the eternal paradise awaiting her after the Rapture, and then proceeded with the ritual Baptism. Is she now a believer? Scully laughed heartily. "Not me. I'm still an atheist even though I did 'technically' accept Christ," she said, using air quotes.

"Of course I feel a little bad. But who's really getting hurt here? My Baptist buddies are thrilled that I'm saved. It would have hung over every conversation if I hadn't accepted Him, like when I wouldn't get a tattoo with my old girlfriends in Syosset. So awkward. Now I know how to talk the talk and we can keep having these nice coffees and playdates and, seriously, you gotta try that Tater Tot pie. Can't find that in the East Village! And since nothing happens after you die, no one's ever going to find out, right?"

❖

"Breast-feeding Nazi" Really a Nazi

Suburgatory, USA—A "Breast-feeding Nazi" is an actual Nazi, combining her fierce lactivist advocacy with her membership in the American Nazi Party.

"You know who is really behind the formula industry? The Jews. Why don't you hear this on the news? The Jews. Why can I only buy my organic meat here at Whole Foods rather than hunt for it myself, as my White ancestors were able to? This one is a trick question. No, just kidding! It's the Jews again!"

Janie Tipton is a young mother with four children under the age of seven who believes that "Aryan Americans" need to repopulate America. This is one of two key tenets of National Socialism: the struggle for Aryan racial survival. "We believe in the Fourteen Words," said Tipton, while searching the Whole Foods aisle for sprouted grain bread. "The Fourteen Words are this: *We must secure the existence of our people and a future for White children.* And I personally would add six more: *Breast-feed your babies, lazy White bitches.*"

How did her involvement in the American Nazi Party lead to her breast-feeding activism? "Oh, you've got that backwards. The breast-feeding came first. After I had my first son, I became possessed with the power of natural birth, and saw that there was only one true, pure method of feeding your child: at your breast, and nowhere else. Anything less is a corruption, a defilement. I became frustrated with my lactivist sisters who were too accommodating, too easy on those weak and inferior bottle addicts. And the more I investigated who was enabling the addicts, I finally discovered the real enemy of breast-feeding: the corrupt Judeo-Capitalist system."

Does her husband believe as she does? "Oh yeah, he is just trying to make enough as a money manager for a few more years and then we'll move back to the land to unchain ourselves from this horrible suburb, the teeming savages right across the town lines, and from the Jew-gamed agri-business industry poisoning our bodies and babies."

Tipton is disturbed by the casual use of the term "Breast-feeding Nazi" to refer to anyone with a harshly judgmental attitude toward bottle feeding. "Some of them think they're all badass for saying 'You should need a prescription to feed your baby formula!' You know what's badass? Telling bottle addicts to turn over their White babies to people who actu-ally *care* about their *health* and *future* and freedom from allergies, their *strength* and *purity* and *intelligence*, which is what we will base our educational system on in our National Socialist future. If you don't believe that, stop patting your-self on the back by calling yourself a Breast-feeding Nazi, get out of the way, and let a real White woman handle this."

The other tenet of the American Nazi Party is social jus-tice for the White working class. "Of course, I believe that the White working man is now nothing more than a wage-slave, tax-cow, and cannon fodder, with their White babies forced to suck off the teat of the Jew-controlled formula-industrial complex," said Tipton.

"The only problem with this one . . ." she whispered, "is that I grew up in [the posh Connecticut suburb] Darien, so it's a little hard for me to talk the talk on the working man stuff, you know, The People of the Folk, and all that. And not to be a total bitch, but I have such nice teeth compared to my White brothers and sisters who believe as I do. So, yes, I really am the 'Aryan from Darien!' But you know, we hated Jews there, too."

◆

SHOUT OUT

I Am Certified Not Muslim . . .
And I Love Your Feminine Area!

Dr. Vijay Singh is a Harvard-trained gynecologist who practices at the Marley Street office building.

Greetings, gentle townswomen! I am passionate about your genital and reproductive health and have been trained at the finest institutions, including the Harvard Medical School. Despite my proven commitment to ladies' health, there seems to be some confusion about just who I am.

I am a doctor first, a Sikh second, and certifiably not a Muslim. Sikhs are not Muslims. Trust me, Muslims are as strange to me as they are to you! I do have brown skin and I wear a turban, but I am not Osama bin Laden coming at you with a speculum, like some of you seem to think I am! And remember he is dead anyway. A turban is not a message that says, "I'm about to kill you, infidel American." It's just part of my religion and identity. I don't look at all those baseball caps everywhere and think Red Sox Nation is coming to get me, even if it sure seems that way sometimes.

Now to be fair we Sikhs have our terrorists, too, like the Muslims—one of them killed Gandhi's daughter! That probably didn't sound very good. But really, don't you ladies know that we *all* have crazies in our shared genetic pool? I don't see the British throwing cans of spotted dick at every Irish person they see. So yes Sikhs have terrorists, too, but none of them has ever hurt an American that I know of. Those were just a teeny handful of Muslim crazies that killed Americans, and I just happen to look like them! I am part of the 99.9 percent of nice, boring, not-Muslim Sikhs out there.

In light of the many recent incidents involving ladies seeing my turban and immediately walking out, I am forced to change my cancellation policy. Now that my not-Muslimness and nice, boring qualities are on the public record, you will be charged a fifty-dollar cancellation fee if you decide I am too scary to do your pap smear. For those of you who are fair-minded and can see that I am simply a Sikh who just happens to look exactly like Mohammed Atta and wants nothing more than to keep your insides pink and shiny and healthy, I hope to see you in stirrups very soon.

◆

Bar Mitzvahs by Shiksas

So! You married a Jew! Maybe fifteen years ago or so? It was your Irish-American mother's dream come true. "Don't marry some Irish stumblebum, find a Jew. They make wonderful husbands. They never cheat. Just avoid the ones named Spitzer, Weiner, and Madoff." Gosh, how did Mom know that? Because she's Mom, of course, she knows everything!

But your little not-really Jewish son is almost a man. And that shiksa in you wants a little representin' at his upcoming bar mitzvah. That's where Bar Mitzvahs by Shiksas comes in! Founded by goy goddess extraordinaire Erin Goodwin-Gotbaum, our team of experienced shiksas will show you how to slip your cultural touchstones into the event with only the barest ripple of, "Oh, that's the shiksa wife at it *again*." Well, it's your not-really Jewish child too, right?

At **Bar Mitzvahs by Shiksas** we can make sure that "Danny Boy" and "When Irish Eyes Are Smiling" just, you know, accidentally pop up on the DJ list. And of course we'll have the bar fully stocked. What is with these Jews and their constitutional inability to get down to business and *drink?* Quite the cross for them to bear, it seems.

For the Italian American, rest assured that Old Nonna Carnivale's gravy with meatballs—pork, beef, and cheese meatballs, of course (are there any other kind?)—will suddenly appear on the catering tables. Oh, those kosher guests will never know the difference. Or if they do, they'll think: *Boy, these Italians might be a bunch of thugs but they sure know how to make a meatball.* Nonna Carnivale's meatballs will put that horrible, bland *kreplach* to shame! And don't be alarmed, Jewish friends, when never-before-seen *paisans*—local guys from the shiksa's own corner of the Old Country—just show up. Because the meatballs are *that good.* And like Jews, paisans stick together.

Or what if your heritage is just a bit . . . trashy? Now for you, no event is complete without Pigs in a Blanket, but your adopted Jewish community might find that a bit . . . déclassé, and your Pigs sure as hell aren't kosher either. Well, as we say quite often at **Bar Mitzvahs by Shiksas:** Tough titties! You, as the shiksa mom, let your child go unbaptized and now he's probably going straight to hell after death—Jesus, Mary, and Joseph. The least these people can do is eat your Pigs in a Blanket! And with our help, very strong encouragement, and well-toned Shiksa biceps, they will. Oh yes, that's a promise.

So call us at **Bar Mitzvahs by Shiksas!** You can take the girl away from the goys, but you can't take the goy out of the girl. Embrace it, shiksas! And of course, mazel tov to your wonderful

7

bar mitzvah boy and his loving, attentive, totally faithful, moral, and stone-cold sober Jewish dad.

◆

Town's Sole Goth Couple Wins Over Hearts, Minds

Suburgatory, USA—The only teenage goth couple in town, once considered an oddity or even a menace, has won over local citizens with the intensity of their devotion to each other and their lifestyle.

"Boy, that's a lot of velvet. They're like one tangled up unit—oh my God! Look, you can't see their feet! It's like they're floating. Floating weirdo Siamese twins," said postwoman Julie Serra. She had just delivered mail to resident Frieda Graber. "I didn't even know there still *were* goths. I remember way back, that guy with the black hair from that gloomy rock band but then when I saw he got fat, I thought, Well, *that's over.* You can't love food and hate life, right? Hypocrite. But these kids, I think they're for real."

The couple, who go by the names "Thanatos" and "Sylvrefyre," first came to be known at Wagner High School by their refusal to separate during the school day.

"These two were a couple of losers before they found each other. They were sad plus scary, to be totally honest. Like, maybe not Columbine scary, but . . . you know, like small- to medium-size time bombs. And now look at 'em."

Principal Gary Briscoe gestured to the couple, who were sitting silently on the basketball court, tracing invisible tear lines down each other's faces. "Seriously, have you ever seen love like that? So yeah, I made some accommodations for them. I let them stay together and let 'em out of gym. Violates their 'beliefs' or whatever. And look what they gave me!"

He fumbled under paperwork and produced an ornate pendant. "They told me it's . . . where's that Amazon slip . . . here it is . . . It's a . . . 'Vladeptus Black Rose Gothic Pendant,' a 'stealthy bat who guards the rose noir, whose perfume reeks of death.' $14.95, on sale. Not bad. Now, I thought that was really thoughtful of them."

"I bet the sex is out-of-this-world great, too," the principal said quietly, apparently not realizing he was on the record. "Wait, do goths have sex?"

Parents who thought it was a phase that would end with the school year changed their minds during the summer heat. "I saw them walking all the way to Dunkin' Donuts . . . in August. All cloaked up and crazy and all. I mean, a goth in August? That's commitment," said Seena Murray. "It's a little sad because I remember Ashley—sorry I mean *Sylvrefyre*—when she was little and she was so pretty. I can still see that face, though, no matter how much of that insane makeup she puts on."

The couple tries to speak as little as possible, but did issue a written statement: "We are thankful that the doomed, beautiful, and terrible people of this town have embraced us, and in return, we will honor their life essence long after their corpses begin their spectacular, eternal rot."

The one citizen *not* won over by Thanatos and Sylvrefyre is thirty-five-year-old Gina Hartnett, a former goth herself, who serves the couple at Dunkin' Donuts. "Oh, please. I hated life before those brats were even born," said Hartnett. "They'll be at one of those fancy weirdo colleges like [nearby] Hampshire College before you know it." Hartnett traded her goth getup for a Dunkin' Donuts uniform several years ago, after running out of tuition money for Green Valley Community College when her father was incarcerated for meth production. "You want to really understand the excruciatingly awful pain of being alive? Spend eight hours making Coolattas. And go home with donut smell that won't wash off. Try that for a few weeks, posers."

◆

"Funny Racist Lady" Enchants Prominent Black Townsman

Suburgatory, USA—A woman couldn't contain her racist statements when encountering a black dad in town today, but rather than finding her offensive, the dad found her to be delightfully funny.

Kellie Alda is a kindhearted and irrepressible mother of two who is so disturbed by racism that when she actually interacts with a person of another race—which is rare in this community—she can't stop herself from injecting her darkest racial preoccupations into the conversation.

She first saw Deshaun Watson and his daughter Amahlia while standing next to them at the annual marathon.

"Oh hi! Good morning!" she said, holding the hands of her twins, Peter and Emma.

"So . . . What's a black guy like you doing in a place like this?" she asked, laughing nervously.

Watson stared at her quizzically. "Just showing my daughter the marathon."

Five-year-old Peter looked up at Watson very gravely and said, "Are you a jigaboo?"

Alda's hand went to her mouth. "Oh my God! Peter! How mortifying, I'm so so sorry. I've been trying to teach Peter and Emma about the history and legacy of racism, which is a hugely important issue to me, so I was telling him all the nasty names for brown people that they should never use: sambos, coons, coloreds, negroes, blackies, jigaboos, jungle bunny, macaca, and you know, the big one, the N-one."

"Yeah, Peter, you might want to forget those other words and just stick with 'black,'" said Watson.

After a few moments, Alda leaned over and said, "I hope seeing this doesn't bother you."

"Seeing a marathon?" asked Watson.

Alda said, "Well, maybe I'm just really sensitive to race, but it's like a white power rally to me. There's a few black people being chased by an army of white people. I mean, I know it's a marathon and all but doesn't it look a little weird to you? Like they're out to run down and lynch those poor Kenyans? Not that these Kenyans are poor. I'm sure they are rich in Kenya—I've seen them running on National Geographic—I mean—oh my God—I mean, on ESPN. They don't wear shoes, but it's by choice—better for running I guess! It's not that they can't afford it, hahahaha."

Alda never asked Watson what he did for a living, because, "I would just never want to ask a black gentleman what he does for a living. I mean, you don't want to make them uncomfortable if they aren't working, or doing something, you know, well you know, *something else.* This guy did seem kind of like a Mr. Mom. Which is great because, you know, black guys aren't always so great on the dad thing let's be honest. . . . What a fine man."

Later on, she saw Watson again at the park with Amahlia. Their familiar greeting attracted the interest of other park-goers. "Those moms are whispering and trying to hide their pointing! How disgusting, how utterly disgusting," said Alda, convinced the other park-goers were racists. "A white mom and a black dad can't talk to each other without thinking about, you know, interracial porn? No, even worse, I bet they are thinking about Civil War slave porn, which is the sickest thing I've ever seen. It was so dirty and wrong and I just can't ever get it out of my head . . . and that slave's upper body, wow, just wow. . ."

Watson beamed at her in sheer amazement. "Wanna come back to my house? We're going to get takeout," he said.

"Gee, well, hmmmm," Alda thought. "Of course!" She whispered to this reporter, "How could I say 'No'? He'd think I was scared of him, but I wasn't, of course!"

As she put the address in her car's GPS, the system began guiding her away from the park and her own relatively mod-est neighborhood, and slowly but surely the houses got big-ger and bigger until they pulled up at a gated house–complex of no less than twenty-thousand square feet, in the exclusive Westgate community.

"Oh wait," Alda said. "Is this guy a manny [male nanny]? But the kid is black, too. Could she be an adopted child of a white family? How many white families choose black babies . . . not that many . . . isn't that awful? What horrible people there are in this world. Wait, could his bosses be . . . gay men? Hmmm."

But as Alda walked in, she slowly passed through a hall-way lined with dozens of pictures of Watson in his NFL uniform, a picture here with Bill Clinton, there with Bono and Nelson Mandela. "Ohhhh. So that's why the people in the park were looking at us? Not because you're black but because you're famous?" Alda said.

"Well, probably a little of both," said Watson.

By this reporter's count, Alda had said a dozen moderate to appallingly racist things. Did it bother Watson?

"No! She cracks me up. Though not sure about my wife. Kellie's the first person in town who's even said the word 'black' to me. She just says what the rest of them are thinking and you can tell she's a sweetheart. Nicest racist white lady I've met in a long long time. Who clearly doesn't know shit about football, but that's gonna change. She's getting season tickets."

◆

Mom Gives Up Pubic Hair for Lent

Suburgatory, USA—An area mom is giving up pubic hair for Lent and can't understand why others don't see this as perhaps the most appropriate choice to honor the suffering and death of the Lord Savior Jesus Christ.

"I mean, I've never done it, but my husband just mentioned it to me offhand. I know it will involve the flaying of my most sensitive flesh and then very itchy stubble and ingrown hairs. Now if that suffering doesn't bring me closer to knowing what Christ went through on the cross, well, I don't know what will," said Polly Tanner.

When Tanner told her "small group" of Women of the Word at church of her decision, most seemed stunned and suggested other possibilities such as giving up Starbucks or gossip. "Ha! Not giving up that last one!" Tanner winked. "I really pushed back on them and said [husband] James fully supported my decision. In fact, James even said this to me, 'I would love you even more than I do now, if I saw how much strength you had in giving up pubic hair to honor Christ.'"

Regina Clark, known as the most cynical of the church group, said, "Riiiight. Your husband wasn't actually *pushing* you toward this idea?"

Tanner said, "Of course not! I've heard ladies take it all off and I've thought about doing it and giving up my pubic hair in the past few years. But this year, I really felt God nudge me on my shoulder."

Clark said, "You know I love you, Poll, but you're gonna get a 'nudge' the likes of which you will *not* believe, and it's *not* on your shoulder."

Tanner replied, "Yeah and isn't that horrific pain what Lent's all about?"

As she made her way to the appointment, Tanner talked about how she has always liked to take good care of herself to honor her Creator, whether it was through maintaining her hair, nails, or teeth. She thought the time had come to add her pudendum to the list.

"It's disgusting down there, to be totally honest. Like a hairy smelly swamp monster," Tanner said.

Doesn't God accept her this way?

"Well, smooth, hairless and clean, that's how I was born right? It was only after I turned into a totally out-of-control trashy sin-crazy teenager that the hairy swamp monster appeared. I'm returning myself to God's original innocent, perfect vision."

Tanner chose the salon where she normally gets her hair cut. She had requested that Cristina, who emigrated from Guatemala, do the waxing. "When they don't speak English, it's like they're not even here," Tanner whispered. "I just thought it would make things more, you know, socially comfortable."

Cristina warmed up the wax and asked Tanner what exactly she wanted.

Cristina: *Brazilian?*

Tanner: *What? I'm* American.

Cristina: *Clean? You want clean?*

Tanner: *Oh yes, clean.*

As Christina began to apply the wax and started ripping, Tanner let the hot pain wash over her. "Wow. Regina sure wasn't kidding." The waxing continued in speedy fashion and tears began to collect in Tanner's eyes. She said, "This was the right thing to do. I really understand suffering, better than I ever have."

Once she was mostly finished, Cristina asked Tanner, "The back? You want the back, too? Backdoor?" Once again, Tanner was confused. Cristina struggled to explain that she wanted Tanner to get on all-fours to touch up the buttocks area. "Your husband, he like the butt?"

Tanner said, "What? I'm doing this for God."

Cristina just shook her head and muttered "*Pinche gringo pendejo,*" which translates to "fucking American idiot."

When Polly walked out, James Tanner was waiting for her. "Oh my God!" said Polly. "James never comes to pick me up at the salon! Look, he's so proud of me."

◆

Petty Crimes Private Investigator

Ever wonder why that girl you used to work with and had no apparent problem with wouldn't friend you back on Facebook? Or why your child wasn't chosen for the status-team in your town's soccer league? Oh, and what about when your idea for the PTO fund-raiser was ripped out from underneath you? What the fuck was *that* all about? If it all sounds petty, but you just can't rest till you get an answer, then it sounds like a job for us at **Petty Crimes Private Investigator.**

Don't call us at **Petty Crimes Private Investigator** if you've been involved in a crime, a domestic dispute, or anything that might end up on a permanent record. That's not what we do. We tackle those maddening mysteries you think about maybe a few times a year, but that consistently bug you when you *do* think about them.

Our investigative techniques include light interrogation, Facebook and Twitter "stalking," and perhaps some subtle playground or playing field observation. We can charge you less, because our private investigators are not those fancy "prestige" gumshoe PIs. If they were, they'd be working on real crimes! But you probably won't even come close to real crime in your lifetime anyway. It's the little things that matter to you, and at **Petty Crimes Private Investigator,** we sweat the little things right along with you. And don't think our PIs are pushovers just because they don't have the "prestige." Many come straight from war zones after exciting and previously litigated stints with the private security firm Blackwater! They'll make quite the impression on the playground, you can be sure of that.

So the next time you ask yourself that bedeviling question, "Why did that bitch from spin class pretend she didn't know me when she cut me in line at Starbucks last week? What the fuck was *that* all about?" call or e-mail us at **Petty Crimes Private Investigator.**

◆

Lesbian Hamsters "Just Grew Apart"

Suburgatory, USA—A pair of lesbian hamsters has apparently separated, a development that has united a family once divided over the same-sex couple in their home.

"We are all crushed. First, Ellen and Anne, then Rosie and Kelli, then Melissa and Tammy, and now Trixie and Fuff, members of our *own family*," said Flora Greenbaum, a longtime supporter of gay rights. She added, "Lesbian break-ups hit me hard. I mean, if lesbians can't make it, who can?"

Not everyone in the Greenbaum household was pleased, at first, to see the hamsters growing close. "My home is a judgment-free zone—you know, like Planet Fitness. All shapes, sizes, and backgrounds welcome at Chez Greenbaum!" said Flora.

But her husband David was not so welcoming. "Two days in, Hannah came running in and said 'Look, Daddy, Fuff and Trixie are hugging like crazy!' And it didn't stop.

They were glued to each other. Now, I'm a reasonable guy, I voted Obama. I'm not some homophobe, but no, I did not think my daughter needed to see that kind of thing at her age. And no, I was not going to have a 'conversation' about it either. And did I want the neighbors to come in and see two girl hamsters dry-humping each other? NO."

Flora Greenbaum vehemently disagreed, and returned the hamster cage to the house after David tried to put it in the garage. "I thought this was a great teachable moment for Hannah and I told David he can kiss my ass. I told Hannah that if a girl hamster falls in love with another girl hamster, they should have the same rights and freedoms and opportunities that *all* hamsters have," Flora said, as Fuff frantically clawed the sides of the cage.

David tried to blunt this advocacy by challenging the very idea that Fuff and Trixie are actually gay. "Think about it this way. Fuff and Trixie are actually in *hamster prison*. They have no one but each other. Do you think all those guys on that show *Oz* were gay? No! They had no choice but each other." David thought about that for a moment and then added, "Wow, you don't think Fuff was raping Trixie, do you?"

Despite David's reluctance to embrace the hamster's sexuality, he was slowly won over by their fierce devotion to Thor, Fuff's son from a previous relationship. "Don't even go near Thor—they'll totally turn Seal Team Six on you, I'm serious. I mean, they're better parents than those loser slackers we never see at Hannah's soccer games. You know, if hamsters had soccer you can bet those lesbians would be at every single game, cheering every single goal without fail. So yeah, I'll admit, I was a little sad when Trixie and Fuff started drifting apart."

That happened, the Greenbaums say, a few weeks ago. Fuff started burrowing in the cedar bedding of the cage's right corner, while Trixie shuffled around listlessly and just leaned next to her wheel for hours on end. The only time their energy level seemed to increase was when they cared for Thor, separately, apparently trying to keep things as normal as possible for him.

Today the Greenbaums finally decided to take them to the vet. "I heard they give cats Prozac, so who knows what advancements there are these days for hamsters and mental health," said Flora Greenbaum. They explained the situation to Dr. Phoebe Macul. Dr. Macul looked a bit perplexed and said, "I think you might be a bit confused. Hamsters are usually sold from the same litter. Trixie and Fuff are surely sisters. And Thor isn't Fuff's son—Thor's a girl and also their sister, but she obviously was born small and didn't grow any hair, poor little thing; they shouldn't have sold her to you. Actually, I'm shocked their mom didn't just eat Thor. Anyway, I'm happy to hear Trixie and Fuff were getting along, a lot of times hamsters tear each other apart. Even though they are drifting now, you've actually lucked out."

The Greenbaums nodded silently and after a pause, David said quietly to Flora, "Sisters? So this was . . . incest?" Flora responded, "Oh my God, like *Flowers in the Attic*. It's sort of sad and sick but sweet. . . ." When Hannah Greenbaum asked, "What's incest?" Flora began to respond, until David raised his hand and said, "Don't. Even."

◆

Toddler News Junkie Thinks Glenn Beck Is Kids' Show

Suburgatory, USA—A four-year-old news junkie recently helped Glenn Beck deal with the Mad That He Feels, something he learned from the late legendary child educator Mr. Rogers.

Jamie Baker watches various news programs with his mother and believes the newscasters are his friends. He especially likes Glenn Beck's show, which—because of its occasional use of props, cartoons, and puppets—he believes to be a kids' program. With Beck's "cozy" sweaters, as Jamie puts it, he even seems like Mr. Rogers. "But Mr. Rogers doesn't get mad and then cry like Glenn does," said Jamie.

"Yeah, I sort of think it's a kids' program, too," said his mother Tricia Baker, who is a Cultural Studies Professor specializing in Marxist and post-Marxist Teddyry. "I watch everything, including Fox News. No, *especially* Fox News. That's how I got pretty obsessed with Glenn Beck. I can't believe I am actually paying money to him now that he's off Fox and has this web-only thing. But it's nuts, totally crackers, and I just can't look away from that train wreck."

"Glenn! Glenn!" said Jamie, as his mom began playing his nightly web program on her iPad.

But the child's face darkened as Beck began to discuss "the people who hate America."

Jamie: *What's wrong with Glenn tonight, Mommy?*

Tricia: *He's mad again, Jamie. You know when Mr. Rogers sings about "What Do You Do with the Mad that You Feel?"*

20

Jamie: *Yes!* "*Do you punch a bag? Do you pound some clay or some dough? Do you round friends for a game of tag?*"

Tricia: *Well, Glenn is working on using his words like you do at school, to get out the Mad that He Feels. He has a lot—a lot—of Mad he needs to get out.*

Jamie: *Mommy, he is talking about "fascists." What's a "fascist"?*

Tricia: *Glenn is, honey.*

Jamie: *But he doesn't like fascists! How could he be one?*

Jamie petted Beck's head on the screen. "It's OK, Glenn. It will be OK. Everything will be fine!" Beck's commentary continued to escalate in intensity, until he abruptly shifted tone and began to tear up and cry. Tricia leaned out of Jamie's earshot and said, "You see? You couldn't make this shit up if you tried!"

Jamie was troubled. "Don't cry, Glenn! Ask your mommy for snack! Maybe you should go tinkle. You'll feel better!" After a moment or two, Jamie said, "Oh look, he's OK. He's calming his body. Yay! 'Adventures of Spooky Dude!'" Adventures of Spooky Dude is a cartoon that features financier George Soros, to which Jamie asked, "Why doesn't Glenn like Spooky Dude, Mommy?" Tricia said, "Because Spooky Dude gave a billion dollars away but not to Glenn." Jamie took this in. "Oh. I like it when he gets out his blackboard or sits on his desk. He's just like you, Mommy. A mafessor!" At that, Tricia snorted. "Riiiight. Just like me. Professor Goebbels."

So if she views Beck as a fascist, why does Tricia let her young son watch him? "Yeah it's a little nuts, I know. In my house, Jamie watches either news or kids' programming produced before 1980. And *only* kids' programming produced before 1980. Have you ever seen *Dora the Explorer*? As in actually sat through it? Talk about a fascist."

◆

SHOUT OUT

Casey Anthony Was Always Guilty by Reason of Eyebrows

Maureen Bentley is a mom and part-time accountant who lives on Stratford Street.

Like every mom in America, I was disgusted and appalled by that "Not Guilty" verdict in the recent Casey Anthony let's-dump-my-toddler-who's-getting-in-my-big-slutty-way trial. Now I'm not some fancy lawyer or anything, but I've seen more than my share of *Law and Order* episodes, and I am mystified that the jury showed a complete disregard for what I saw as the clearest evidence of her guilt. And that was her intense devotion to eyebrow hygiene.

I'm really not a snap judgment person at all, and in fact I have served with integrity on several juries, including one where we sent a glue-huffing scumball to prison for burglary.

But the first time I saw that mug shot of Casey Anthony, I didn't need to see any more "evidence" beyond those over-coiffed eyebrows. I knew she was guilty as sin. No normal mother would have a daughter go missing and think to herself, "Hmmm, gee, my eyebrows are looking a little shaggy, better touch them up in front of my lighted mirror!"

Not to say that her eyebrows looked good. My eye-shaping genius Irina shuddered when she saw that mug shot because of how that "mom" butchered those eyebrows! Then the whole eyebrow thing got even crazier during the trial where she seemed to go on some wild, uneven plucking orgy. Here she is, still worried about her brow arch, while sitting in jail *not* potty training little Caylee and *not* waking up in the middle of the night, exhausted and pissed off like the rest of us worn-out mothers who don't kill their babies?

Come on, jury! A woman still worried about those brows while "grieving" a dead toddler? If that was me, my eyebrows would be as big as Borat's mustache. Frida Kahlo would have nothing on me! Why? Because I love my children and I'm not some piece-of-trash whore and neither are any of my friends. There have been times now and again when I've let myself go, you know why? Because I was too busy running myself ragged being a *great mom.*

Rule of Law and Reasonable Doubt my ass. Get your act together, American Justice System, we're supposed to be a beacon of sanity around the world. Next time, look to the eyebrows.

◆

"Intactivist" Mom Celebrates Area Foreskins

Suburgatory, USA—A local "intactivist" mom has formed an unlikely alliance with a gay man who fetishizes the "uncut" penis.

"Circumcision is barbaric, an all-out human rights atrocity that we are inflicting on the most helpless among us," said activist for "genital integrity" Tara Cote. "At first I was just plain angry. I put a homemade sticker on my car with a slogan: PEOPLE WHO CIRCUMCISE AREN'T PLAYING WITH A FULL DICK. But a lot of people honked and gave me the finger."

Cote said that experience made her change her tack. "Instead of guilting parents, I'm trying to show how natural and beautiful the foreskin really is. I'm still judging them, of course. I just don't tell them." Isn't that hypocritical since Cote admits she had her first son circumcised? "No! I was uneducated, uninformed. There *was* no movement when I deformed my baby. Well, now there's no one that can say, 'I didn't know.'" Cote's "reeducation," as she calls it, came after her involvement with an influential Facebook campaign called "Fuck You, Keep Your Babies Whole."

While trying to dispel the notion that foreskins "are stinky," "collect cheese," and "look sad," Cote stumbled upon websites that glorified the foreskin, for example "Uncut, Uncensored" and "Hooded Heartthrobs." From this, a fruitful political partnership was formed. "I found some fringe groups, but after I started chatting with them, they were talking about how vicious the Jews are and how they are controlling the world, it was really scary. So I'm so glad I found Libearache, which is what he likes to be called in the—what did he call it?—the 'bears, cubs, and chubs community.' Don't call him Donald. He gets really mad, but that's his real name," she whispered.

Libearache explained his advocacy. "You know when I'm in my comfort zone with my cubs and chubs, I talk about how succulent and fragrant a ripe, unwashed foreskin can be. But out here when I find these moms and moms-to-be, I just talk about how foreskins are God's creation and all that bullshit. And how circumcision is cruel and horrible and dangerous. Which it *is*."

When some mothers asked Cote about Libearache's fetish-wear, which Libearache toned down considerably for his suburban audience, Cote replied, "Um, he's just . . . a motorcycle enthusiast." Some moms were also disturbed that he was approaching pregnant women, saying, "May the foreskin be with you!" But others found Libearache an engaging presence, with Cote adding, "He can be a real chatty Patty when he wants to be and loves looking at the latest gossip on TMZ. He's fun!"

Cote is confident she and Libearache can convince moms of the horrors of circumcision even if they, like her, have already chosen it for their first child. "We can save the next one," she said. What about the growing body of research suggesting circumcision reduces rates of STD transmission? "Oh, yuck! Look, gays are the only ones who really have to worry about that stuff and my kid's sure as hell not gonna be gay."

◆

And you can bet your bottom dollar "Monsieur Fitzgerald" at school won't have the balls to risk all that politically correct censure and teach the swagger-speak your child really needs. That's where **Swagger-Speak International** comes in! Our swagger-speak is taught by a veritable United Nations of tough-as-nails nannies and au pairs from around the world. And trust me, they love hurling these phrases at your bright American child; we barely have to pay them! No matter where your children choose to do their overseas college application-builders, they'll be armed with phrases like these, when visiting a pub or jostling for position in a train ticket "queue," or on that African eco-safari!

In Polish:
On jest zasrany skurwysyn.
He is a shit-covered bastard.

In Mandarin:
Ciao Ni Zu Zong!
Fuck your mom!

In Swahili:
Mshenzi we!
You savage!

In Japanese:
Omae no Kaasan Sakana kusa.
Your mom has a bad fish smell.

In Russian:
Chto b ty provalilsia, mudak dolbanyi!
May you fall through hollow cunt!

In Swedish:

Ursäkta mig, men din fitta syns.

Excuse me, but I can see your pussy.

In Spanish:

Me Cago En Su Puta Madre.

I shit on your whore mother.

In German:

Du Saftsack.

You stupid bastard.

In Tamil:

KandaraOli - Cun-daara-Olee.

Slut . . . who sleeps with anyone.

In Arabic:

Air il'e yoshmotak.

May you be struck by a dick.

Now, as a concerned parent, you might fear that these phrases will get your child in a bit of trouble. And yet we've only had two "international incidents" . . . and consider the outcomes! One of our students got to meet Secretary of State Hillary Clinton, and the other now has his own Wikipedia page! Think how impressive *that* will look for college admission. And isn't the small risk of a modest scuffle worth the pride that your child will feel as an American who stood up to an uppity foreigner on his *own turf* and using his *own language?* It's like the bluster of George W. Bush plus the globe-trotting know-how of Barack Obama. Call us at **Swagger-Speak International.** And remember, if you ever meet a real America-hating fuckwad in Bucharest, repeat after me: *Sa-mi bagi mana-n cur si sa-mi faci laba la cacat.* That will say to him, "Stick your hand in my ass and jerk off with my shit." Now that'll show him who's boss!

◆

Woman Shops at Wal-Mart to Feel "Pretty, Thin"

Suburgatory, USA—An affluent local woman chooses to shop at Wal-Mart, not because of the low, low prices, but because shopping there makes her feel "pretty" and "thin."

"Just get a look at this place! I'm like a total rock star here!" said Terry Gotlieb, who often feels inferior in her regular social circle at both the Temple Beth-El Sisterhood Social Group and the Junior League, because of what she calls her "fat giraffe body" and unmanageable "Jew-fro."

"I just feel so relaxed and energized when I come in here. I can let it all hang out and still feel like a million bucks. "Hey, Fred!" Fred Upton, one of the store's many senior citizen employees, is Gotlieb's favorite Wal-Mart greeter. "That guy, he's the best. He knows all my kids' names. Always says, 'Hi Sunshine! You look beautiful today.' You know, Fred has to take two buses to come work in this shithole?"

Upton, taking his break sitting in the store's blood-pressure testing stall, was asked for his impression of Gotlieb. "Fat? She thinks she's fat? In my day, Terry'd be called a 'tall drink of water.' I think she has a fine figure. Don't know where she gets 'fat' from. She's the most beautiful Jew I've ever seen. But she's a sad lady, too. Her values are a little cuckoo in the head. You know, when I talk to her, I always feel so much better about my own life. So I love it when she comes in."

Gotlieb believes that the diversity in the store lends her an advantage no matter the looks of the other shoppers. "Even the best-looking Puerto Rican girl is no match for an average white lady like me. I'm coming out on top every time." Gotlieb paused. "Except for J-Lo. But I don't have to worry about seeing J-Lo at Wal-Mart, do I?"

Gotlieb marvels at the number of children some of the patrons of Wal-Mart have, and the impossibility that they are saving for the future. "Oh God, if these people don't start saving, their kids will never have what I have. They'll *have* to shop here. Not like me, just here for fun."

Gotlieb particularly likes the pharmacy section, where she feels "the thinnest and the fittest." Here, Gotlieb observes, "I see all these gigantic obese people with diabetes buying crap for 'wound care' and oh grossssssss. I am so lucky."

Gotlieb uses the Wal-Mart pharmacy, not because it's cheap, but because, as she puts it, "I don't have those cunts from the Temple hanging over me seeing me pick up my Zoloft and Ativan." Do her friends know she shops at Wal-Mart? "Are you out of your fucking mind? They'd think we were being foreclosed on. Or they'd bitch I was an 'enemy of the people' or something for shopping here. Well, unlike *them*, I actually *know* people of different colors and different backgrounds, like Fred, because I go to Wal-Mart."

Gotlieb had never heard of the popular website Shoppers of Wal-Mart, where contributors surreptitiously photograph Wal-Mart shoppers for the amusement value. On this reporter's iPad, Gotlieb began clicking through and laughing. "This is *great!* Oh my God, look at that," referring to a photo of an overweight African-American woman's loose back fat.

"I've totally seen that, like, a million times." But her mood darkened when she arrived on a picture entitled "The Old & The Frizzy-full," which showed Gotlieb on an especially bad hair day, slack-jawed, speaking to Fred Upton.

Gotlieb abruptly ended the interview and began walking out. A checkout girl said, "Terry, you haven't paid yet." Without turning around, Gotlieb thrust her hand behind her and said, "I don't have to pay for anything here." Upton said goodbye as Gotlieb left the store unchallenged, but got no response. "There goes my sunshine," he said.

◆

Home-Schooled Girl Excels in Competitive Spelling, Blow Jobs

Suburgatory, USA—A home-schooled girl excels in championship-level spelling and blow jobs, with both skills giving her local renown. "Thanks to my amazing parents, I have the confidence and commitment to excellence that I would have never had if I spent years as a slave to an educational system that creates kids who can't think for themselves, who have no real love for learning, and know nothing about the life of the mind," said sixteen-year-old Catherine Busby.

At a very young age, Busby says, she knew exactly what she wanted to accomplish. "Memorize words to win or at least place in the biggest contests and get on the news, and, separately, to get boys to like me. So I dug in, and dug in hard."

"Did she ever!" said Paul Minnow, seventeen, one of Busby's early boyfriends—a starter project in her quest to perfect and master her blow-job skills. "I can't believe she dumped me. If I was her 'training subject,' I can't even believe how good Catherine is now. Those guys seriously must faint."

Another boy expressed his pride at her success at age fifteen, coming in third in the Scripps National Spelling Bee. "I mean, *appoggiatura? Autochthonous?* How does she know this shit? But I have to tell you, when she is up there and thinking really hard and then starts that slow spell, letter by letter, the excitement building and building, all I can think about is my cock in her mouth. Then when she gets it right? Oh my God, it's explosive. Even her dumpy outfits turn me on now."

Busby's family members describe themselves as "neopagan" and believe they honor The Goddess by purchasing only secondhand clothing. Why didn't they give their daughter a more traditional pagan name? "Oh, we were psycho yuppies in the '80s and '90s."

Busby's mother, Sophie, is very proud of her daughter's spelling accomplishments, and has little problem with the fact that she has earned the nickname "Blow Job Babe" by local boys. "First of all, I trust Catherine's judgment without reservation. She spent years on my breast, and years more learning right at my knee. I'm convinced we gave her the security to express her deepest desire, coupled with the wisdom to do it responsibly and with integrity. Who am I to say that achievement in sexual ability is worthless? It's a skill she can utilize and enjoy her whole life!"

While she seems equally skilled in both spelling and blow jobs, the spelling holds a more sentimental place in Busby's heart.

Says current boyfriend Jonah Klein:

"I tried to get her to spell out one of her crazy words on me with her tongue, but she wouldn't do it. She said 'Spelling is sacred.' I had to settle for 'Heartbeat of America,' where she squeezes me, like thump-thump." Klein demonstrated a pulsing grip. "Thump-thump. Thump-thump. And that was fine, too, of course. I really respect her!"

So where did Busby learn all these techniques? "Oh God, the Christian home-school girls of *course*," referring to the kids she meets with regularly for home-schooling field trips and other enrichment activities. There is often tension between the neo-pagan and the Christian home-schoolers, but Busby made fast friends. "Oh, they're lovely! And they are like blow-job ninjas. But, well, not to be mean, but their spelling is for shit."

◆

Dr. Drama

"When life hands you a problem, let's make it more interesting!"

Dear Dr. Drama:
One of my best friends, I'll call her "Meg," is being emotionally abused by her husband, I'll call him "Brad." He berates her, controls her, and has made her a prisoner in her own home. She's so under siege she can't even imagine leaving. I'm desperate to find a

*solution and to force her to get help. I'm at my wit's
end!*

—Hopeless in Suburgatory

Dear Hopeless:
In my many years of online training to become a clinical "psychologist," while not slaving away in that awful call center, I learned the technical term for men like "Brad." We old pros in the biz call them Asshole Dickwads. Now, Dr. Drama doesn't want to be a Debbie Downer here, but the fact is research shows that the recovery rate for Asshole Dickwads is extremely low. You know what's even lower? The chances that doormat "Meg," living under siege with an untreatable Asshole Dickwad, will do something about it. So that leaves you, and if this is a hopeless situation, I always say, why don't you have a little fun with it? Someone should!

I like to give clients action items to achieve their goals. So here goes: First, sabotage him at work. You wouldn't believe how easy this is, I know firsthand! Find even one coworker and start feeding him shit about your Asshole Dickwad. In the age of social networking, we'll have Asshole Dickwad the talk of Twitter before you know it.

Second, contact your friend's dad. Just because "Meg" says, "He'll kill Brad if he finds out what he's doing!" Hey, that's no skin off your back or hers. What do you care if Asshole Dickwad gets the shit beat out of him? I have four words for you: It's about fucking time.

And finally, start rocking that passive aggression you always wanted to use, face-to-face, with Asshole Dickwad. Trust me, your beaten down friend can't do it, so it's up to you. Maybe you can demean his career choice: "Oh, I've heard that field is the least competitive of the fields you could have chosen, and there's a lot less money, and your peers are really not the brightest, but I'm sure the quality of life you have is so worth being in that really not-competitive field." Or "Yes, the kids are a bit... large. But you must love that they're so like you!" He will smile, but inside his rage will burn with the intensity of a thousand suns. Enjoy!

◆

Mom Befriends, Infuriates Mormon Missionaries

Suburgatory, USA—A local mother has based her entire social life around a pair of young missionaries from the Church of Jesus Christ of Latter-Day Saints, but she has unwittingly alienated them with her ignorance.

"If she offers me Starbucks one more time, Oh. My. Heck." said Buck Berkeley, age twenty, of Salt Lake City, Utah. Berkeley is spreading the message of the Book of Mormon with his companion or "comp," Cason Mabry, twenty-two, of Harris Landing, Idaho, in what is known as "tracting," or door-to-door proselytizing of selected suburban neighborhoods.

"Case, how many times have we told her about the coffee? Six times? She couldn't give a scrud about our eternal damnation. I mean, has she ever heard of Wikipedia? It's not that hard to figure out that we can't even get near her gross coffee."

Berkeley was referring to Kim Ballante, forty-one, the mom who first greeted the young men at her door two months ago. "Aren't they just the cutest?" she said.

Ballante says she has learned much from the pair about the tenets and history of the Mormon faith, including a description of the angel that adherents believe visited church founder Joseph Smith in the late 1800s. "Moroni was the last Nephite prophet, whatever the hell that means, and then his angel wrote the Mormon Bible on golden plates?! Can you be-leeve this shit? Mo-RONE-eye. Buck said it's spelled like *moron* with an 'i.'"

Berkeley laughed when this was mentioned to him. "She had no clue I was calling her a moron. She just kept going 'uh-huh, uh-huh,' and 'wow, that's so interesting!', which is all she says when we actually try to give her the Word of Wisdom. One day she kept calling Joseph Smith, *Robert Smith*. Remember that, comp?" Cason said, "Yeah, because she loves that old creepy band The Cure. Man she is so old." Buck agreed. "So so SOOOO old."

On this day, Ballante welcomed the boys in and said, "You're just in time for 'Hot Topics!'" referring to the topical portion of the show *The View*, which they frequently watch with her. "I thought they would like Elisabeth [Hasselbeck]. She's all religious like them. But they don't seem to like her. She wears a cross, and they don't like crosses, these people. Like, like vampires or something, they are seriously scared of them."

At the end of *The View*, Ballante said, "Ethan [Ballante's two-year-old] is still sleeping! You know what that means . . . Appletini Time!" which apparently meant she would mix up some drinks for herself, even though the young men are forbidden to drink alcohol.

"*Sex and the City*," Berkeley said quietly to Mabry when Ballante went to prepare her Appletinis. "Do you think she got

Appletini Time from *Sex and the City?*" Mabry asked, "What's *Sex and the City* again?" Berkeley said, "You know, that show from when we were, like, twelve, and those movies? Those trashy old bags running around New York drinking and having sad sex and all? The women in this town pretend it's, like, real or something. It's kinda tragic. . . . They just need *real love* from their husbands. What is wrong with these men?"

After Ballante consumed several drinks, she lost her inhibitions with the young men, whom she believed secretly found her attractive. "Come on, you know you want more than one wife. Admit it! I'd totally be a sister wife if I could have Bill Paxton! But not that creep from *Sister Wives.*" Ballante was referring to the polygamist husbands on the HBO show *Big Love* and the TLC program *Sister Wives.* She gets most of her knowledge about the Latter-Day Saints from the shows, and more recently from what she's read about the Broadway send-up, *Book of Mormon.*

Berkeley, as the more senior missionary of the two, handled the polygamy question. "Ma'am, our Church disavowed polygamy more than a century ago. While there are some fringe groups who continue to practice polygamy, they do not represent the people or beliefs of our Church in any way, shape, or form. I will have one wife, and we will be together with our children forever."

"Holy shit, you are so adorable," Ballante said. "Alright, alright, alright. But you need to at least give me something," Ballante said, leaning in closely to the young men, who were visibly apprehensive.

"Show me your magic underwear. We read this book in book club about crazy Mormons and they were talking about magic underwear."

Mabry cleared his throat and said, "Ma'am, they are temple garments that we wear at all times to remind us of our sacred covenants. Other religions like Judaism also include special garments in their faith."

"Jeez-us, you guys are all God and no fun. It's gonna be a long long life for you two if you don't loosen up. Trust me on this," Ballante said.

After leaving the home for the day, Berkeley said, "You know, the thing that kills me the most is that she is so pathetic that she sits around day after day with a couple of twenty-year-olds and she thinks WE are the freaks." Mabry nodded in agreement. Ballante confirmed this impression. "Yeah I love those boys, but of course they're freaks. They're Mormons knocking on doors! If that's not a freak, I don't know what is."

So why do Mabry and Berkeley keep going back if they feel both offended and hopeless at their chances of getting Ballante baptized? "Oh, I don't know, maybe because I'm-With-Stupid?" Berkeley said, gesturing to Mabry. "Case, like an idiot, let it slip to our Zone Lord [the mission supervisor] that this woman loved us and now they are convinced they have a golden." "Golden," they say, refers to an easy conversion target.

Mabry added: "I don't even want her at this point even though we look like rock stars if we get her dunked [baptized]. I don't give a fudge about her or her soul—but if she becomes LDS and has a celestial marriage, then that poor guy she's married to and that kid she totally, completely ignores, are going to be stuck with her for all Eternities."

◆

Ice Cream Man Assaulted Because He's the Ice Cream Man, "Not Because He's Muslim"

Suburgatory, USA—The dads who admit to the harassment and second-degree assault last month of Egyptian-born ice cream man Suleiman Rahman insist they did not attack Rahman because of his faith, but because he's the ice cream man. They also say he is a "possible perv," a "rolling extortionist," and a "kiddie-poison pusher." But they claim they have no problem whatsoever that Rahman is a Muslim, and argue this incident, which involved pushing and yelling, does not fit the definition of a federal hate crime.

"That's straight-up slander!" said Mark Watson, one of the accused parents. "We aggressively suggested the ice cream man leave the school parking lot last month because we are fed up with him and all the problems he causes, following families all over town, ruining every nice event!"

Janet Maroney said Rahman's truck arrives just as the kids begin playing soccer, making it impossible to keep the kids on the field and forcing parents to bring cash to every game. "I feel like every time I see that stick-up truck headed for me, I can kiss five bucks goodbye unless I want an epic meltdown. Then if a friend forgets her cash, I say buh-bye to ten bucks."

Jodi Keyes wishes she could say no when the ice cream man arrives but doesn't want to look like a "joy-sucking cheapskate" or one of those "granola moms." Peggy Davies is proud to call herself a "granola mom" and even she can't resist buying her kids what she calls the "frozen death on a stick" with "neon gumball eyes." "Yes, I'm granola, but I hate a tantrum just like the rest of you," Davies said.

Others alluded to what they see as a corruption of this classically American institution. Some who asked to remain anonymous thought Rahman was "a Gypsy or something" and mourned the days when ice cream trucks were manned by "wholesome teenagers" and not "old possible pervs who don't even live in town." One wondered, "Does he sleep in there?"

Parent Roger Jackson asked, "Have you heard that toy piano tune his truck plays? It will seriously haunt your soul. It's like Satan on four wheels." And these feelings have nothing to do with the fact that he's a Muslim? "I said *Satan*, not *Osama*, didn't you hear me?"

So what does Rahman say about the incident? "In 2002 I was held for three months by the Egyptian secret police. You think these homosexual-looking men scare me?" After some cajoling, Rahman admitted that he didn't think town residents hated him because he's a Muslim, even though his lawyer is pursuing a hate crime charge. "I don't think they even knew what I *was* before this happened. I think they just thought I was the poor brown stranger taking their money and annoying them with my tempting and delicious ice cream. They blame me because they can't say no to their spoiled-rotten children. So no, I don't really think they hate me because I'm Muslim. But I couldn't really blame them if they did. Because I definitely hate them because they're American."

Wolf Blitzer—
Live From the Lactation Room

Suburgatory, USA—This is Wolf Blitzer. And you're in . . . the Lactation Room. We have a situation developing in the Lactation Room at the Unum Provident office building today, as two mothers battle over their degree of virtue and commitment to pumping breast milk for their babies.

Jill Branson is trying to convince Susan Markle to "tough it out," "don't be a quitter," and "remember all the troubles formula-fed babies have," as Susan struggles to produce enough breast milk. For those of you unfamiliar with the process—as I was before I discovered this oasis of feminine splendor—working mothers use electric pumps and then store their breast milk for their babies to drink later. We go to the fight playing out live.

Jill: *Breast-feeding for me has been excruciating, bloody, and by far, the most important and life-fulfilling job I've ever had. I know it's a gift that I'm able to do this. Susan's wavering commitment is an insult to those who can't breast-feed at all, even though most women can, if they try hard enough, and* care enough.

Susan: *Like Wolf? He can't breast-feed. What if he was a gay man? He and his husband couldn't breast-feed.*

Wolf: *Ladies and gentlemen watching out there at home, to clarify, I am not gay.*

Jill: *Well, gay Wolf and his partner could get donated milk. I'd donate to them! But really, I'm most interested in women and what women are capable of doing.*

Susan: *Of course you are! Wait, you think people would just take your milk, no questions asked? Isn't that like letting your kid have unprotected sex with a stranger? Hey, why is Wolf Blitzer in the Lactation Room with us?*

Wolf: *Because I'm a breast man. I told you I wasn't gay.*

Jill: *Wolf, my breasts are for my* baby.

Wolf: *Sorry, Jill. I'm not made of stone.*

Jill: *Well, anyway, I nursed through multiple nipple cracks and nipple psoriasis, thrush, a kidney infection, an abscess, a shattered elbow, major surgery with my first son, and a ruptured appendix. I don't think* anything *can stop me from breast-feeding. I willed every last damn drop out of my body.*

Susan: *Why don't you take up another kind of competition that will pit you against other women, like a marathon? Women's roller derby? Probably get some gore there to brag about, too.*

Jill: *I'm not competing with you! I just want what's best for* your child!

Susan: *You don't even know my last name! THAT'S IT! I'm going up to the roof to SMOKE. Did you hear that, Jill? Going to report me to protective services? Michelle Obama?*

Wolf: *While the First Lady is a vocal supporter of breast-feeding, I should note that the President himself struggles with smoking.*

Susan: *WhatEVER Wolf, what are you really adding here?*

Ladies, I will add that, like the First Lady, I'm also a big supporter of breast-feeding whenever and wherever a beautiful, luscious, ripe new mother chooses to do so. And if you're done pumping, my work here is done. I'm Wolf Blitzer, and you've just been in . . . the Lactation Room.

◆

Mom Unaware of Two American Wars

Suburgatory, USA—An area mom is unaware of two American wars fought over the last ten years.

"Huh? What are you talking about?" asked Carol Stewart. "And I can't talk for long, I've got Tommy's soccer pickup at 3:30 p.m., have to swing back and pick up Sarah from Mindy's house, then get all of us to the store. Jesus, that sounds like absolute hell, doesn't it?"

This reporter explained to her that 9/11 had led to a "war on terror" that still has US servicemen and women in harm's way in both Iraq and Afghanistan. Had she heard of 9/11? "Now that is extremely insulting. In fact, 9/11 touched me close to home. I actually saw it happen. Live. They pre-empted *Regis and Kelly* for it. So just back off with the 'hey-ignorant-Mommy' line of questioning." Arriving at the soccer field, she said, "Get in the van, Tommy. *No.* You've had enough ice cream. No. *Now.*"

But is she aware that the United States went on to fight two wars after that?

"Here's what I know. I know that we went into Afghanistan, found the smoking gun mushroom cloud WMDs, thank God, did that amazing rescue of that adorable blond soldier girl—poor little thing. Then Seal Team Six got al-Qaeda's top guys—Saddam, bin Laden, Qaddafi. Then George W.

Bush did that whole thing on the boat with the big WE WON! sign, and Axles of Evil were finished. See? I know a little something about something besides Mommying." She looked satisfied as she retrieved Sarah from her playdate. "Thanks, Mindy. Did she behave nicely, I hope?"

As she headed to the store, this reporter told her that major combat did *not* end with the MISSION ACCOMPLISHED sign, and in fact had gone on for years, costing a trillion dollars. She was still quite dubious.

"I haven't seen Ken Burns do anything about it. I guess you're going to tell me you know more than Ken Burns? You, some small-town suburban reporter? And if there were really two wars, wouldn't I know someone who had gone? Hellooo! And wouldn't every house have a flag out?" Not necessarily. Since the military is all volunteers these days, it attracts mostly lower- or middle-class recruits, and those who have no connection to those socioeconomic groups would be almost fully insulated from the impact of two wars.

"So I guess you're asking, 'Where've I been?' Oh, I know, raising the future of America."

Did she want to know the number of American servicemen and women and civilians killed in the two wars?

"You know what?" she said, exasperated with the questions and all three of her kids yelling or throwing things across the minivan. "I've got my own army to worry about. Sorry. Priorities."

◆

SHOUT OUT

Toddler or Anchor: I Report, You Decide

Linda Mendes is a former TV news producer turned stay-at-home mother who lives on Rice Street.

I take to the Shout Out today because I know a lot of moms leave their jobs and think, "All I know how to do these days is wipe a baby's ass and listen to a baby scream!" Well, I'm here to tell you that if you can handle that, you can handle a challenging career in TV news! Getting both crapped on and screamed at by anchor babies is what it's *all about.*

OK, I exaggerate. An anchor never did literally crap on me, as my son did many times. But metaphorically, yes, my friends and I were crapped on with alarming regularity.

So here's a ten-part puzzler for those moms out there who don't think they have what it takes to work in TV news. Trust me, after dealing with a child, you probably have the chops, as you will soon see. So, am I describing my toddler or one of the many anchors (or reporters) I've worked for or worked around or heard about from colleagues over the years? I report, you decide.

Question #1. This person broke wind, frequently, loudly, shamelessly. This person also, how might I put this delicately, often mined for the mother lode, usually at the same time as the aforementioned wind-breaking. Toddler or Anchor?

Answer: Anchor. *At least my tiny boy had some shame. Frank would tell the lunch crowd at Applebee's, "Excuse me, I farted." This particular anchor just said "Welcome back to the show!" And my toddler, mercifully, lacked the fine motor skills to flagrantly pick his* nose. *This two-fer of anchor farting and picking would happen during commercial breaks, eliciting a chorus of "Oh gross!" "He's at it again!" and "Is he done yet?" in the control room.*

Question #2. This person was nicknamed "Cranky Pants" by his caretakers. Toddler or Anchor?

Answer: Anchor. *As in, "Watch out, Cranky Pants hit traffic, his BlackBerry crashed, he just saw that we tanked in the last quarter-hour ratings, and he's on the fucking warpath."*

Question #3. This person was a huge admirer of the sober, thoughtful reporting of *NewsHour with Jim Lehrer* and watched it religiously. Toddler or Anchor?

Answer: Toddler. *My toddler loved when Jim "Ware" used to "wee-cap" the news at the end. When the show would list servicemen and women killed in Iraq and Afghanistan, Frank would say "Jim Ware is sad now." He also loved substitute anchor Gwin Eye-full, and analysis by David Bwooks from the* New York Times. *He's really mad Jim Ware retired. Crazy-mad.*

Question #4. This person's caretaker had to remove carrot shreds from his lunch because he "hates orange food—no orange food!" Toddler or Anchor?

Answer: Anchor. *Though, to be fair, Frank didn't like orange food either.*

Question #5. This person was inconsolable when told he couldn't have a monkey as a pet. Toddler or Anchor?

Answer: Toddler. *OK, you guessed it; that was my three-year-old. Most anchors care a tad more about their crucial demographics than they do any living creature, other than themselves.*

Question #6. This person struggled mightily with language development. Toddler or Anchor?

Answer: Anchor(s). *One of my proudest moments while driving around suburbia was when Frank heard a public radio anchor say rapprochement, and he repeated it flawlessly. But with reporters and anchors? Some have left us writers and producers awestruck at their ignorance. It's also a very delicate dance as a writer, whether to spell out a word phonetically for the "talent," because if it's a word or name they know, that's you effectively telling them, "Hey, boss, I think you're a moron!" But if you didn't put the "prono" in, and then they prove themselves to be morons on live television, then you, the writer, get ripped a new one, and a big new one at that. I polled TV friends for favorite prono mistakes. Here's a sampling:* Remember the Alamo: *"Remember the a-LAMB-o."* Fidel Castro: *"Feye-dell (like Fido) Castro."* Mao: *"Mayo."* Pneumonia: *"Puh-numonia."*

Question #7. This person turned a very angry red, balled up his fists, and screamed when he was read something he didn't like. Toddler or Anchor?

Answer: Anchor. *My toddler had things he didn't like to read, but at least he didn't crumple up the offending material and throw* *it at me. He also didn't know how to say "Who the FUCK wrote this?"*

Question #8. This person has trouble looking into people's eyes. Toddler or Anchor?

Answer: Anchor(s). *When the camera is on? No problem. With the staff? Not so great on the eye contact. Thank goodness this wasn't my toddler, because I definitely would have worried about autism.*

Question #9. This person whipped out his penis any chance he got. Toddler or Anchor?

Answer: Toddler *and* **Anchor(s).** *With apologies to my sweet boy for violating his privacy, my toddler son loved showing us his "nudie rudy." (Blame entirely his baby-talking mama. When he was streaking around the house, I started calling him a "nudie rudy." He eventually decided that his penis was actually called a "nudie rudy.") As for the anchors, well, their nudy rudies were deployed in far less innocent circumstances, and just like the maids and the butlers in a secretly steamy English manor, we, the news-servants of the all-powerful, knew a lot more than our masters ever suspected.*

Question #10. This person just up and ran away from his caretakers, leaving them terrified and heartbroken. Toddler or Anchor?

Answer: Anchor. *Actually, the above isn't completely true. The anchor did just disappear without warning, not showing up or calling in for days, weeks, never to return. But we weren't terrified* *and heartbroken. In fact, we had a lot of fun in the newsroom during that time and some nice relaxing lunches.*

As I review my puzzler, I realize I better snuggle on down in this crazy suburb I now call home and get cozy, because I'll probably never eat a nice lunch, or produce TV, in that town again. But that's OK. I'm happy with the less-than-relaxing lunches I now have at, yes, Applebee's, with my little ball of energy who tells me he loves me ten times a day. I never got that with an anchor. Frank can crap on me all he wants.

◆

Mom Crushed to Learn that Facebook Isn't Job

Suburgatory, USA—A local stay-at-home mom who calls herself the "Facebook Queen" was crushed to find out, after nine months of avid social networking, that Facebook is not a job and she won't be getting paid.

Molly Brooks, thirty-eight, has become an instant legend among her 732 Facebook friends for seeking and accepting friend requests from people she doesn't know, or barely knows.

In a very short period of time, Brooks has made herself a fixture, by being the first on anyone's Wall to offer birthday greetings and by invariably being the first person to "like" a status update. Her response time leaves her friends awestruck and a bit concerned.

"Seriously, my update will be fourteen seconds old and she's already lunging for it," said Patrick Mulleavy, who knows Brooks through a one-time fraternity party hand job back in college. "It was great," he said. The hand job? "No, no, my fraternity. I miss that life so much. Thank God for Facebook. Reconnecting with Molly brought me a little closer to those memories."

He considers Brooks's Facebook prowess similar to her approach to a hand job. "A little too eager, a little forced, but total A for effort," said Mulleavy. "She was a really nice girl in college, and from what little I can tell from Facebook, she's turned into a really nice lady and mom. With maybe not a whole lot going on in her life."

Other friends worry that her Facebook vigilance means she is neglecting her family responsibilities. "How does she keep up that totally insane pace with the liking and the commenting, the 'Get better soon!' and 'How fun!' and still watch her kid? He's only two years old!" said Maura Tanner, a childhood friend.

"Molly's like a sister to me and I've known her in *real life* for decades, which is more than I can say for these other 'friends' she has. 'Shahgan Vatan'? His Facebook page says he's a Pakistani mariner. Did you hear that? A PAKISTANI MARINER," said Tanner, disturbed that Diehl would be wasting her time with what she called "some rando across the world."

Tanner explains, "Molly met him in . . . the Jewish Maritime Historical Society page on Facebook. I mean, what the FUCK. I'm not sure what's weirder—a Pakistani who joins the Jewish Maritime Historical Society or a stay-at-home who's a) not Jewish, b) barely ever been on a boat, and c) gets history from, like, going to see *The Help*. Molly watches that one stupid movie and she thinks she marched on Washington arm in arm with MLK or something."

Brooks says she joined the Jewish Maritime Historical Society "because it looked cool and my friend Herb asked me and he just had a baby, Henry. Isn't he soooo cute?" She thumbs her iPhone to find the pictures. Does Brooks feel, as some of her friends do, that she's wasting her time and life on Facebook? "Well no, of course not. I do get paid, you know. Though Facebook is apparently total crap with their payroll, since I've been on nine months and still haven't gotten paid. Gotta get on them for that."

This reporter then explained to Brooks that she must be confused, Facebook is not a job. As she let this information sink in, Brooks looked as if she was going to cry. "I can't speak for a little bit," she said. Instead, she updated her status on Facebook. "Molly Brooks is the world's biggest moron. All this time I thought Facebook was a job and was going to pay me. Feeling like the most massive loser. :("

But before Brooks could even finish typing, her update was flooded with comments. "Molly = The Awesome." "MB, don't go changin'!" "Molly—I may not 'know you' IRL, but you were the ONLY person to say something when Aunt Lucille died. XOXO." And from Shahgan Vatan in Pakistan, where he was apparently on Facebook at 2:00 in the morning his time: "Molly, when I tell my friends that they are wrong, when I tell them that the US does have good and kind people, I say, let me show you Mrs. Molly Brooks of America."

With that, Brooks did indeed begin to cry and said, "I guess Facebook taught me what really matters in life. It's not about the money. It's about real people and real community. . . . OK, I need to direct message Shahgan—his third wife was having some huge fibroids removed yesterday."

◆

Teacher Says What She Actually Thinks, Infuriates Parents

Suburgatory, USA—A local teacher, fed up with the media and the public attacking her profession and union, has stopped sugarcoating things, infuriating parents with her brutal honesty.

"These parents think teachers have it sooo easy? That our union is not much better than a bunch of public-sector gangsters?" says fifty-six-year-old teacher Lily Peterson. "Well, I have two words for them and they start with an F and a U. It's high time they hear exactly what I think of some of them and their precious babies."

And so the weekly PTO meeting was replete with stories of the teacher's disturbing candor. Instead of being told to schedule more outdoor activities for her son, Missy Carter was asked, "Are you really going to let Blake eat himself into type 2 diabetes?"

Sarah Martin admits that her son has had a few behavioral incidents, but offers that "the cat healed up just fine."

She was flabbergasted when, instead of offering strategies for encouraging appropriate behavior, Peterson simply told her, "Hide your knives, and lock your bedroom door at night."

Alexandra Petit, whose son is an outstanding student, but also a loner and an obsessive "deep thinker," also got some troubling honesty. Peterson told Petit, "Your kid's either Bill Gates or the Unabomber. It could really go either way." Petit says, "I'm really clinging to the Bill Gates thing and trying to forget the rest, so can we just not talk about it?"

Her comments were also a mixed bag for Tracy Heffernan and her daughter Erin, as described by Peterson.

"Yeah, I told Heffer that Erin is an annoying tight-ass, but she's super bright and bossy and I wouldn't be shocked if she was another Hillary Clinton. I'd probably vote for her but she's still kind of a stuck-up tool."

Heather Lee says her daughter Bella is a lovely child and that she was never told anything of note other than that Bella is "very anxious to please, no matter the consequences." At the latest teacher's conference, Peterson clarified what she meant: "She's going to be the girl giving group blow jobs at frat parties if you're not careful."

But Peterson is quick to point out that she loves many, if not most, of the kids, especially Vincent Stone. Peterson says Vincent is "unusually mature." When his mother—whom Peterson describes as a "no-good slacker"—said thank you, Peterson shot back, "You deserve exactly no credit for it."

As is the case with Stone's mother, Peterson notes that it's largely the parents she has the problem with, not the kids.

Robin McIntyre—another parent irate about the teacher's decision to be honest—wouldn't reveal what was said to her, though Peterson was happy to oblige. "Oh, I'll tell you exactly what I said to her. I said, 'I know you're hungover and tired from banging that sleazy boyfriend of yours, but get your kid's ass in here on time.'"

Peterson sits back, looking both satisfied and energized. "Maybe I shouldn't retire after all."

◆

Family's A-Ha Moment: All Uniquely Devastated by Oprah's Departure

Suburgatory, USA—Each member of the Houlihan household, in their own unique way, is devastated by the departure of American talk show treasure, Oprah Winfrey.

These days, at 4:00 p.m. two-year-old "Little" Cathy Houlihan walks around the house, listlessly looking for Oprah, and banging the TV. "Black Mommy? Black Mommy? Where's Black Mommy? When Black Mommy coming? Is she coming back?"

"I know it's awful to watch, isn't it?" said Cathy's mom, "Big" Cathy Houlihan. "But at least Little Cathy has hope that Oprah's coming back. I have to live with the knowledge that she's not!"

Big Cathy explains Oprah's impact on her life. "Oprah taught me everything I know about being a white lady! I mean, that didn't come out right at all. She taught me what it meant to be a mom in America. A mom who lives in her own truth and has a sassy black friend to give her the kind of down-home Southern advice she needs. And sometimes that advice meant accepting things I wasn't raised to approve of. I did what Oprah told me, and I'm a better person for it," Cathy said.

"And thank God, I mean, thank *Oprah* for that," said Houlihan's now openly gay teenage son, George, who's also in mourning for Winfrey.

"I might have killed myself had Oprah not made my mom believe that it was OK for me to be gay. FUCK those people who pick on Oprah. FUCK. THEM."

His dad, Ian Houlihan, has his own reason for bemoaning Oprah's farewell, but at this point it's a secret. "I'm gay, too, and I was hoping she would do a few more of those shows on closeted gay husbands to, you know, help ease the blow to Big Cathy. "The Wrath of Cath," we call it, it's a scary scary thing. So, no hope for coming out anytime soon. Thank god for gay porn. I'd probably kill myself if it wasn't for gay porn."

Ian's father, Walter, who lives with the family, is apparently the only straight male in the household, but the ladies he prefers are the black ladies. "I can't believe my Ebony Goddess is gone."

Did he have a problem with her weight? Walter was nonplussed. "In my day, youngster, women were a lot . . . roomier, like Oprah. Boy, I used to love watching her, imagining all the wonderful zestful steam baths I might have had with her, her dark black gorgeous flesh glistening with sweat. . . . that smile lighting up every afternoon with her wit and beauty. . . ."

Even the children's live-in nanny is missing Winfrey. "Just to be clear," said Elvira Martinez. "I don't like the blacks. Even the rich blacks. Especially the rich blacks. But Oprah gave me one whole hour every day of peace and quiet without this whole house of babies needing something."

◆

SHOUT OUT

Act Like *Grown-ups* at the Drugstore

Eliot Dubin is a concerned pharmacist at the Bartlett Pharmacy on Cabot Street.

I had hoped I would not have to take to the public Shout Out forum to address certain behaviors we are witnessing at the

Bartlett Pharmacy, but the health of our patrons and the dignity of our workers must take top priority.

First, calling in prescriptions you don't pick up.

Now I know that Maria Osnos really can't predict when her nervous collapse will occur and when it will ease. I know that Bill Sanford sometimes looks down at his painful toes and thinks, "Well, as the youngest person ever to have gout, maybe I should do something about both my lifestyle and this excruciating pain." But then Maria's nervous collapse goes away after a half-dozen glasses of wine, or Bill decides he just can't rouse his fat ass out of the house to pick up his meds. But all of you should know that when our pharmacist rushes to fill orders that you never pick up, he is putting aside the needs of others. I can only assume that John Maron was able to get the erection he sought without the help of the medication that he ordered because he never picked it up. I give a hearty guy-to-guy *mazel tov* to that, but please, be considerate of our time as professionals.

Second, cutting ahead in line.

Melissa Henry, I understand your urgency in getting your medication last week. I know better than anyone, except perhaps a prostitute, that a vaginal yeast infection requiring prescription medication is quite "a situation" indeed. But to stride so aggressively to the counter that you knocked over Millie Wexler's walker? It is true that Millie uses the pharmacy counter as a place to socialize now that those worthless piece of shit kids, Bob and Sheila, have decided to forget they have a mother and leave her to us. But that means Millie is practically a member of our family now, and no yeast infection, no matter how itchy, steamy, or smelly is worth disrespecting her. At Bartlett Pharmacy, we simply won't tolerate it.

Third, yelling at us because your doctor didn't refill the prescription.

When you are hopelessly addicted to painkillers, like Daniel Chelmsford, it is hard to keep your head about you. When things go wrong, you blame the wrong people. You need to remember, Daniel, that it is the doctor, not us, who has control over your stash. You want your meds? Knock over the store after hours like the rest of you criminal drug seekers, but don't scream at me during my shift.

Fourth, spying on people's medication.

Now this one I really am the go-to expert on. Of course you're spying on what other people are picking up, Jessie Borden. It's completely natural to sit there and use your iPhone to Google the name on the bottle Greg Silver is holding, only to discover that he is picking up medication to block his unstoppable cravings for alcohol. It's human nature! But it is the divine right of pharmacists to know this information and no one else. And we don't even need to Google the stuff, it's all right in our noggins! We dream in medication names!

I hope this clears up some of the poor conduct we've been seeing at Bartlett. We're all grown-ups here. Let's start acting like it.

◆

Child Convinced Being Disabled Rocks

Suburgatory USA—An area child is convinced being disabled "rocks," despite his mother's best efforts to explain the struggles that disabled people face.

"Why can't we park right in front of Starbucks, Mommy?" said five-year-old Mikey Purcell.

"Because that's only for people who have disabilities—who can't use their legs, let's say, as well as we can. It's so they can use the store just like we can," said his mother, Sandy Purcell.

"Hmmmm. That sounds pretty good," Mikey said as he and his mother entered the Starbucks and asked to use the bathroom. The barista told them the regular one was occupied, so he gave them the key for the handicapped restroom. Mikey had never seen one. "Mommy, this bathroom's huge! And so clean. It smells like, like, rainbows and miracles and fruit punch." Sandy began telling him this was because the handicapped restrooms aren't used as much as regular ones.

As Mikey thought about this, he said, "I wish I was disabled."

"No, honey, you don't. Disabled people are people just like you and me, and they matter a lot, just like you and me, but life can be pretty hard for them. It's no walk in the park."

"I know that. You just told me they can't use their legs," said Mikey. The boy and his mom returned to the car and made their way to the Edgewood Elementary School.

"What I'm trying to tell you, sweetie, is that it's not an easy life. If you were stuck in a wheelchair, you could never walk to school with your friends," said Sandy. "But I never do that now," Mikey pointed out. "We go to Starbucks, get your iced chai latte, you play with your phone, and then we ride to school. Hey, if I was disabled could I ride that super cool bus with all those ramps and buttons that go 'zzzhoooop'? The floors move up and down! Those kids are so lucky. Being disabled rocks!"

Sandy Purcell grew somewhat exasperated. "I don't think you're getting it, dear. It's not a cool thing. It's not like being Justin Bieber. I mean, there's nothing wrong with being different and we all have struggles, but it's not something to wish for. You might not be able to talk, like we're doing right now . . . "

He thought about that. "So you could sit criss-cross applesauce on the carpet and not say anything when Miss Barrett says something to you and that would be fine. . . ."

His mother added he might need to be fed, like he was still a baby. "Great!" said the boy.

Purcell finally exploded. "Michael, be happy you're not disabled! I don't want to make it sound awful but sometimes people can't have regular lives at all, like getting married or wiping their own bottoms!"

Mikey went over to his mother right before lining up to go inside for school. He cupped her face in his hands. "But Mommy, you know I'm marrying *you* and you already love me so much AND you still help me wipe my bottom sometimes when I can't reach."

"So," he said quietly to himself, "how do I get disabled? Would it hurt?"

◆

Vegetarian Mom Vexed by Son's Meat-Lust

Suburgatory, USA—A vegetarian mother is vexed by her son's newfound passion for meat and his complete lack of empathy for the animals that, as she puts it, "suffered horribly and died so you can eat a disgusting chicken leg."

Liz Stakun blames a friend of hers who, without her permission, provided her son Max with a fried chicken leg, which he was eating as Stakun arrived at her friend's home to pick up her child from a playdate. "OK—Anne has been undermining me since college. First she horned in on my major, then surprise, surprise, she rushed my sorority. So passive aggressive."

"Hey Anne! Hugs!" Stakun stiffly embraced her friend and tried to hide her horror, as she saw her son tearing into the chicken leg with abandon. "Um, Anne, you know I've been a vegetarian. Since 1994. After the U2 concert where you blacked out. Remember?" said Liz, trying to contain her irritation. "Oh, Liz! Of course I know you're a vegetarian but I never in a million years thought you'd impose your beliefs on a growing boy! And look how much he loves it. How can that be so wrong?"

Indeed, Max was enjoying it so much that Liz had trouble getting his attention away from the greasy chicken leg, which he was examining in a methodical way that he sees on his favorite forensic crime program, *Bones*.

Liz: *Max, do you remember the nice mommy chicken we saw at Landsakes Farm, the one who loved her chicks sooooo much, like Mommy loves you?*

Max: *Oh yeah, they were sooooo cute, Mommy. What a good mommy that hen was.*

Liz: *Yes, but honey, I just want you to understand that what you saw at the farm and what you are eating on this plate are one and the same.*

Max: *But Mommy, they're* dead now *and they're* delicious!

And with that Max returned to dismembering the leg, telling his mother, "Mom, this is the best part; you need to try it." He pulled the chicken meat off the bone. "You're gonna *die* when you taste this, the skin's the best!" he said as he pulled the skin away from the meat. Liz sighed and shot Anne a perturbed look but said nothing more. "Max, we'll talk about this more at home. By the way, I realize we found a pair of bunnies in the backyard."

"Awesome!" said Max, as he wiped the chicken grease off his face. "Are they dead, too?"

◆

Surrogates of a Certain Age

Attention women of a certain age! We know that, for years, in your swinging twenties, you probably thought to yourself with pleasure, *Well, if I ever* really *get down on my luck, I can always sell my bountiful eggs for a tidy sum!*

And when those wonderful glory days came and went, you probably remember reading ads about couples seeking eggs for in vitro and realizing, "What, I'm too old to donate?! No one wants my eggs anymore? My eggs are *worthless?*" This moment can be especially cruel if you were one of those gals who attended a prestige school. You spent years secretly relishing the idea that you harbored golden Faberge status-eggs that could be harvested for top dollar at any time (practically worth auctioning off at Sotheby's, for fuck's sake) and sold off to a couple who wanted their own little Ivy League bundle of joy.

Well, part of growing up is learning a simple but hard fact: Your lady parts lose value. But at **Surrogates of a Certain Age,** we can ease that hard fact with a compelling one of our own: Some parts don't age as fast as others. Your warm, still moist, roomy and inviting uterus is fully usable until age forty!

Yes, you can carry someone else's child long after your eggs have shriveled into oblivion. Talk about grapes of wrath! Well, forget those little old rejects. Our match team will place you with a couple who will pay a little less, considering your advancing age, but who will never make you feel less of a woman, even if you really are.

So why don't you consider doing something wonderful for another couple, but more important, something wonderful for *yourself.*

E-mail us for a promotional package at **Surrogates of a Certain Age!** Proof of age required.

◆

Mother Discovers Russian Au Pair Is Richer than She Is

Suburgatory, USA—An area mom has discovered, much to her chagrin, that her Russian au pair is far wealthier than her in Russia.

"Actually, what's worse is that she's not just richer than me in crappy, depressing Russia. She's richer than me *here, too!*" said thirty-nine-year-old Jen Barofsky.

Barofsky says she chose the eighteen-year-old au pair mostly because of her English skills and her unattractiveness. "Oh please, I'm not stupid. 'eighteen-year-old Russian au pair'?

I don't need my husband sitting back and watching a hot Russian teen romping around here. So yeah, I picked the frumpy one who'd probably be a workhorse and eager to please."

But when Galina Popov first arrived, she spoke little, though her English was near flawless. Popov barely acknowledged the children she was supposed to care for. And she walked around slowly, making small "snorts," as she surveyed the 5,000-square-foot home and the property.

"I mean, at first I just thought it was a Russian thing. They're not exactly the most uplifting people, you know? Maybe that's why they hated us Jews—we're loud and proud, I like to say. Life's not one long pity party, Russia!" said Barofsky. Her husband Jeff started calling Popov the "Crabby Cossack."

When Popov's attitude failed to improve, Barofsky considered that maybe the girl actually *was* an anti-Semite. But in fact it was not anti-Semitism at all. "One day Galina left her Facebook page open, and holy fucking shit. That girl and her life make me look like trailer trash. Who knew there even *were* rich people in Russia?"

Barofsky got to see just what Popov left behind in her native country. "There were pictures of her houses. Houses, plural. I counted at least three. There were hundreds of nightlife shots of her all over the place dancing and drinking, and there were all these dressing-room pictures of her visits to some really swank mall. Still pretty ugly but definitely not frumpy. Nothing like her au pair video at all."

Barofsky decided to ask Popov about it.

Galina: *Well, yes, you do live quite modestly compared to me.*

Jen: *But why didn't you tell me?*

Galina: *I was supposed to tell you that you are far less fortunate than I am?*

Jen: *No, I mean, of course, it's OK that you are blessed with a lot of money. I'm just curious as to why you chose to become an au pair.*

Galina: Chose *this?* [Snort] *No. I'm more suited for [French resort area] Cap Ferrat. But my father is a . . . ran into trouble with an ally of an oligarch, and he thought it best for me to leave my country for a while.*

Jen: *What's an oligarch?*

Galina: *The smartest, fastest people in Russia who were in the right place at the right time when Communism fell.*

Jen: *Oh. Is that why you left all your fancy clothes at home and didn't wear them in your au pair video? You're in hiding or something?*

Galina: *No, my mom told me to do that after we looked you up on Facebook and saw your . . . house. She told me an American woman wouldn't want an au pair who looked richer than her, or looked like she might try to steal her husband.*

Jen: [Nervous laugh] *Hahaha! Now that's just silly.*

Galina: *Well, my mother is grateful you took me and I know she would want me to ask you if you would benefit from some of our . . . what do you call it in English . . . hand-me-downs? We have so many.*

Jen: *Uh, no.* Nyet. *Thank you.*

So did Barofsky keep Popov? "What, and have my dead Bubby rise from the grave and pelt me with boiling matzoh balls? She'd be mad enough that I had the Crabby Cossack living with me, but a *rich* one? It's a *shande*."

◆

Dr. Drama

"When life hands you a problem, let's make it more interesting!"

Dear Dr. Drama:
We are having a battle in town over whether or not to remove a house close to mine on Shelton Street, to make room for a new Wal-Mart. Many of my neighbors are thrilled that they're going to get rid of that house, because a Level 3 sex offender lives there. Now, I'm no fan of sex offenders, but as a person of conscience I would rather have him in town than Wal-Mart, which I believe does things far worse to our commu-nity—collectively—than any one man. I have told no one this, just you, and I look forward to getting some of your sage advice.

—Wal-Not in Suburgatory

Dear Wal-Not:
Sooooooo you would rather have a neighbor who has, say, ass-raped a child than a store that offers rock-bottom prices? Because low prices are bad for the poor? Have you ever been to a Wal-Mart? No? That's because you're not poor!

I know your type, Wal-Not. You just have to have your special mom-and-pop bullshit coffee and ironic old-time-y hardware store that's highway robbery, because you can afford it, and

you think Wal-Mart is the Evil Empire. Well, here's my advice for
you, since you've told no one but Dr. Drama about your troubled
"conscience." Start walking around telling people your views.
And send the medical bills to the ass-raper.

◆

Kid's Book Used to Explain:
Don't Cockblock Your Gay Uncle

Suburgatory, USA—A gay uncle is using the heartwarming book *Uncle Bobby's Wedding* to urge his overly attached niece to stop "cockblocking him" in his search for love and passion.

"I love her to bits, I really do," said "Gunkle" Rob Marino, referring to his niece Ella. "But just like her mom, she thinks I'm her funny gay play toy. But you know what? I'm a human being like everyone else who likes to come home from work, watch Netflix instant play, and get fucked as much as possible by my *boyfriend*. So when I saw this book, *Uncle Bobby's Wedding*, I lunged for it. Yeah, the book is a great celebration of committed gay love, blah blah blah, but to be honest, really I just saw it and thought, *Oh my god, this might just get it through Ella's adorably thick head that I need my life back*. And I need my *own* committed gay love. Like fucking Gunkle Bobby did."

Uncle Bobby's Wedding tells the story of a gay guinea pig named Bobby, whose niece Chloe is troubled when her favorite "special" uncle finds love. Slowly Chloe has to accept that Uncle Bobby is going to marry another special guinea pig, Jamie.

Marino describes how his life as "Gunkle" evolved.

"Oh, this is all her mother's fault—my sister Angie—who I also love to bits but you know, her idea of a gay man is someone to 'be there for you.' You know, cuz I'm gay. I know it's hard for her, a single mom in suburbia? That's almost as bad as being a single gay dude in suburbia. But seriously, it takes me an hour to get out of the city to see them, and it's like I'm on call 24-7, paging Rob to the rescue! Because I'm supposed to be really good at wiping your tears and going to the mall. I do more than that idiot shrink of hers. She should be giving *me* those co-pays she hands over to that woman."

And then Angie had Ella, and gay uncle Rob became the go-to "Gunkle."

"You know, they all assume I have no life because I'm gay, which is hilarious because if I was a whore, and I'm *not*, I could be out every night fucking five different guys if I wanted to. If that's not a life, I don't know what is. My sister always assumes I can babysit or can come over when Ella's loser dad doesn't step up. If she hadn't had Ella, I'd be so out of here. Ella really is the best thing that ever happened to me. I just need more space."

So Rob and new boyfriend Jayson took Ella out for Afternoon Tea at American Girl Doll Place, and sat down with Ella's best-loved "Molly" doll, described by the company as a "lively, lovable schemer and dreamer growing up in 1944." And Rob had his own "Kanani" doll.

"Ella insisted I have one, and Angie chose it because she thought it was really kitschy for me. Why does she think I'm some screaming queen—I hate kitsch! Why does my own sister think every gay man is a screaming queen?"

Rob brought *Uncle Bobby's Wedding* with him to tea and began to explain why nieces need to stop cock-blocking their Gunkles.

Rob: *Now Ella, see, Bobby found Jamie after many many years of being alone.*

Ella: *But you haven't been alone, Gunkle Rob, you've had mommy and me.*

Rob: *Of course, honey, and you know I love taking you to American Girl and talking to you every night before bed and having frozen hot chocolates and everything we do all the time, but at some point, everyone wants to have their own family.*

Ella: *You're my Gunkle! You are my family!*

Ella began crying but Jayson, who'd been quietly assessing Ella, whispered to Rob, "She's playing you. Let's throw money at this."

Jayson said, "Ella, is there something maybe we can get you, something you've been wanting, so that Rob and I can carve some time alone together and it won't be too sad for you?"

Ella carefully composed herself and said, "The new Josefina doll from 1824 on the Santa Fe trail. The whole six-book series. And extra moccasins and shawls."

Jayson said, "Deal!"

As they left tea to go purchase Josefina, Jayson looked down at the first American Girl doll Rob ever bought for Ella, "the lovable schemer," and said, "Wow, Ella's a real 'Molly,' huh?"

◆

Mom Buys Muscle Massager
to Really Massage Muscles

Suburgatory, USA—A local woman was unable to convince the men at the Eaton pharmacy that she was buying a muscle massager to really massage her muscles.

Mary Pickering was first noticed in the orthopedic care aisle where she was purchasing supplies for her elderly mother. Tom Carrothers and Joey Marti, on their break from the construction site down on Milford Street, noticed her and thought she fit the sexual cliché that has run rampant among men of their age: "MILF."

"Hey, Tommy she's pretty MILF-y, huh? Tits are a little droopy, but me still likey," said Marti.

Carrothers said, "Yeah, that yummy mummy's aged pretty well." Pickering ignored them.

But soon Pickering was in the personal massage area and Marti and Carrothers were electrified. As she picked up the Ergonomic two-speed Handheld Massager and began heading to the checkout, they decided they were done shopping and would check out along with her. While standing in line, she overheard Tom Carrothers say, "You know, I have just the thing to 'massage those muscles' of hers. Right, Joey?" Joey said, "Yeah, you know if I had a pretty lady like that at home, she'd be getting her muscles massaged every night, real hard, too. No batteries required!" They laughed and elbow-poked one another.

Pickering turned to the men and said, "Look, I genuinely need this device for my shoulders. My physical therapist told me to buy it." Both men were silent, smiling and slowly nodding with their mouths a bit ajar. As she arrived at the checkout, the clerk, who looked to be nineteen, had the same expression. Pickering said, slowly and forcefully, "I have *sore shoulders*." "Of course! That will work wonders on shoulders. You know, we are also having a special on RePhresh vaginal gel," the clerk said.

At this point, she said, "Little boy, I don't have a dry vagina."

"Yeah, definitely not, no dry vaginas if I was in the sack with her, right?" said Carrothers to Marti, who held up his hand and said, "Don't leave me hangin'!" Marti high-fived him.

Pickering finally lost her composure. "Do I look like a fool to you? Do you really think I would trust my orgasms to a piece of junk I buy at a drugstore? I have a whole goddamn *family* of vibrators at home. *And* a husband who fucks me into oblivion whenever I want. Oh, and could you be any more cliché? 'Don't leave me hanging,' all that MILF and Yummy Mummy shit? Does anyone even still use those stupid terms?"

Marti, looking chastened, said, "In porno they do."

"What are you even buying anyway?" asked Pickering, accusingly. The men dutifully extended their hands: Marti was holding Lamisil anti-fungal cream. Carrothers had Preparation H, and a copy of *Martha Stewart Living* magazine.

◆

Mercedes-Driving Dad Dreams of Easier Life for His Children

Suburgatory, USA—A local dad spoke about the current economic hardship and his hopes for an "easier life" for his children, while getting his Mercedes detailed at the Hooper Street Car Wash & Detailing.

Eric Sellers' S-class sedan had a bumper sticker that read HAD ENOUGH?, which referred to what he called President Obama's "war on the little guy."

"I mean, I am not one of those Tea Party crazies who thinks Obama is a socialist or a secret Kenyan terrorist or anything. I think he's dangerous just because he's an old-fashioned tax-and-spend liberal. The tax rates in this country are criminal," he said, looking for agreement from the mostly Latino men using small brushes on the crevices of the car.

"You know, I'm just a regular Joe, a suburban small-business man. We are the backbone of this economy! And yet I'm expected to pay more than 40 percent of my income to the government. Money that should be going to my kids, who are suffering in this terrible recession. Thank God I have a whiz-bang accountant who can get that 40 percent down to about 10 percent, but that's still highway robbery."

At a 40 percent tax rate, this would put Sellers in the top 1 percent of America's wealthiest individuals. Sellers scoffs at this notion. "Oh please, do I look like Donald Trump? I may be 'technically' in the top 1 percent, but with prices these days I'm really just average like everyone else. Right, guys?" He gestured to the men working, who murmured their approval.

"You know, America used to be great. Everyone had a fair shot. But I don't know anymore, I just don't know. I just hope and pray life is easier when my kids are grown up than it's been for me these last few years. And for them."

He went on to describe some of their recent hard-ships. "This year, I told my wife 'No more Nordstrom. It's

Nordstrom Rack or nothing.' To see her face, oh God, as a man, that was quite a blow. That really hit my dignity."

Sellers has also had to curtail the travel and leisure budget.

"I had to sit them all down as a family and tell them we couldn't go to Vail this year. Our ski-week would have to happen in Vermont. I thought the kids would be sad, but really, they looked terrified. Seemed like a perfect time to teach them about the tyranny of marginal tax rates."

While some give too much, Sellers says, other "protected classes" enjoy outrageous benefits.

"These teachers and their extortionist unions get the whole fucking summer off. Wouldn't you like to have the summer off too, guys?" he said, addressing the detailing crew. "I know I would!"

With his car finished, Sellers checked his iPhone for the time and said, "Guys, not to be a dick here but I dropped the car off at noon and it's 2:06 p.m. Two-hour guarantee?"

The workers looked at him and without saying a word rang up his 25 percent discount.

"Hey, every penny counts, am I right?" Sellers said.

◆

Precious Toddler PR

If you're a good parent, and we know you are, you are convinced that your little Aidan or sweet Isabella is the single most extraordinary, precious child ever to walk this fine earth. But be assured: You are the only one who thinks this. Well, maybe your husband and the grandparents do, too, but that's it.

At **Precious Toddler PR**, we utilize third-party confirmation to boost your incorrect assessment of your child's extraordinary nature. It could be the well-placed comment on Twitter from a seemingly objective observer. Or a preschool "teacher" no one's ever seen before appearing at afternoon pickup to note your child's amazing attributes. **Precious Toddler PR** will create the buzz you believe—again, incorrectly—that your child deserves.

Think of **Precious Toddler PR** as an investment in your child's future. Word of mouth will open doors when he has to go to college. Why not start when he's still in the sandbox? Give us a buzz and we'll give it back, at **Precious Toddler PR**.

◆

PTO Stunner: New President "Not a Power-Mad Psycho"

Suburgatory, USA—Longtime PTO participants at the Burns Elementary School are reeling at news that their new president is neither crazy, nor annoying, nor a "power-mad psycho."

"Oh my God, I'm afraid to say it and end up jinxing it but she seemed completely normal!" said Joellen Joyce. "And. *And.* She told a dirty joke. In front of her kid. And then said, 'Don't tell on me!'"

Joyce is referring to Laura Beazley, who was a dark-horse candidate to succeed Emily Fahdin, the previous PTO head, who was nicknamed "Bin Fahdin." "Yeah, it's stupid, but we laughed so hard after we came up with that one," said Joyce.

As for Beazley, Joyce said, "No one knew anything about Laura so we were convinced that she was a 'Bin Fahdin embed,' that is, an acolyte and pawn of Fahdin, who has moved on to a bigger PTO stage at the Lexington Middle School.

Fahdin was loathed and feared for fomenting dissent, or in PTO parlance, "shit-stirring"; for launching bizarre vanity projects like commissioning a video crew to document her activities for, in her words, "posterity"; for alienating the working parents by calling them "blood-sucking PTO parasites"; and for demanding total control.

Katie Mulheren described one run-in with Fahdin, after Mulheren floated a new, and apparently unwanted, idea for improving one aspect of the school's annual Rodeo Fun Fair. "She trapped me in the spaghetti aisle at the store and got her face right up to mine. I mean, an inch away from my face, and said, 'The Fun Fair has always been done this way, and always will. People in this town don't like change. You need to be very very careful and think really hard about what you are doing.' I really can't do it justice, it was so insane."

Fahdin also policed members for insufficient spirit or irreverence, unless it was directed at working moms, whom she seemed to openly loathe. "Oh you don't need Freud for that one! It's because she didn't make partner at her law firm, and had to plow her type-A crazy into something. Lucky us! It was the PTO," said Mulheren.

So when Beazley scheduled her first PTO meeting, members were prepared for the worst. Here's some of what she said:

"Thanks for coming out at night, I know that's a change for many of you but we need to try to include working parents in the PTO, so they do not feel like PTO pariahs.

My PTO philosophy can be summed up in four words: No Bullshit, No Drama. I believe PTO is for making extra money for things the school can't provide, and offering a reasonable—and I stress the word *reasonable*—number of projects to get families involved in the community or enrich education. That's it. If you, as a working parent, want to kick in a little money, that counts as volunteering, and you will be thanked alongside those fortunate enough to have time to lend their labor. There'll be no guilting under my watch. And while I welcome any and all ideas, I do not welcome cliques or backstabbing. I don't know about you, but I remember high school and have no desire to relive it."

As Beazley finished, it was apparent several mothers were tearing up with relief at this unexpected sanity. Mulheren: "I know it's ridiculous, especially since we had that silly name for her, but this is how I felt when I heard we got rid of Bin Laden. The real Bin Laden."

❖

Principal Replaces Pledge of Allegiance with "Eye of the Tiger"

Suburgatory, USA— A principal has been placed on paid administrative leave after having children recite lyrics from "Eye of the Tiger" rather than the Pledge of Allegiance.

Parents learned of the principal's "lesson" when kids began using phrases from "Eye of the Tiger." At first, they assumed the kids had learned them from Wii's "Guitar Hero" game. But they weren't singing the words, rather, they were reciting them, and one parent contacted the media. "Yeah, that principal was so far out of line, but I gotta say, I do love that song," said parent Richard Dunn, who began humming it himself and lightly pumping his fist.

The principal in question is Jon Bohrman.

"They're making a big deal out of nothing! I was trying, very creatively, I might add, to challenge the kids at Maginn Elementary to pursue their dreams, question assumptions, and think for themselves. That's why I forced them to learn 'Eye of the Tiger.'"

Critics of Bohrman say that was not his sole motivation. They say the answer can be found on his Facebook page, which shows he has "liked" several groups: Ayn Rand Greatest Philosopher That Ever Lived, Ayn Rand Rocks, and Ayn Rand's Breasts. Bohrman flinched a bit at the mention of that last group, but readily admits that that he is an adherent of Rand's Objectivist philosophy, which argues that morality is about the pursuit of one's own happiness or self-interest. Objectivists believe only unfettered capitalism can allow for this to flourish, and in general, believers oppose many or most forms of collective action.

"Yes, I'm a believer. Not in God, of course, but in Objectivism. I got a copy of *Atlas Shrugged* back in college from the really smart guy in my frat, a genius, hedge-fund god now. This is my favorite quote: 'The world you desire can be won. It exists . . . it is real . . . it is possible . . . it's yours.'"

Bohrman thinks the time has come for Objectivism to flourish. "Let's face it, America is in decline. Shouldn't we emphasize to our children the importance of personal drive, of having the motivation to face down detractors and fight another day? Now, *that's* what "Eye of the Tiger" teaches, not the Pledge. Listen. . ." As he played the song, he spoke the lyrics that the kids themselves recited.

'Risin' up, back on the street.
Did my time, took my chances.
Went the distance, now I'm back on my feet.
Just a man and his will to survive.

He muted the song. "Now compare that to the Pledge. All the Pledge does is force kids to mouth empty, robotic promises to be loyal to a nation and a god. Nothing about shooting for the moon. What's that all about? I'm sure if Ayn Rand was alive, she would be a fan of the band Survivor."

When this reporter corrected Bohrman's pronunciation of "Ayn" (he was calling her "Ann" rather than "Ein"), Bohrman paused for a moment and said, "The liberal elitist media is the reason I'm on leave in the first place, instead of back in school where I belong. But I take solace and get my drive from Rand's own words: 'The question isn't who is going to let me; it's who is going to stop me.'"

"I'll tell you who's going to stop him. You're lookin' at him," said Superintendent Phil Troutman. "But of course, the union will try to save him."

Doesn't Bohrman see the irony that a union—a collective organization loathed by many Rand believers—is making sure he is still getting paid and will try to fight his dismissal?

"Oh, not at all. Being in the union is in my rational self-interest."

◆

The Totally, Completely Not-Creepy Chimney Sweep

Now, ladies, we all know when you get that loud knock on the door, you're thinking, *Oh no! Is that the chimney sweep? I forgot that I made that appointment and now I'm* barely dressed! *Where, oh where, could my clothes beeeee?* Well, if you enlisted our fine professionals at **The Totally, Completely Not-Creepy Chimney Sweep,** you have absolutely nothing to fear!

At **Totally, Completely Not-Creepy Chimney Sweep,** our serviceman will not size you up and down and think about all the dirty things he wants to do to you. **The Totally, Completely Not-Creepy Chimney Sweep** will never ask to use the bathroom just to look in your medicine cabinet in hopes of learning more about you.

The **Totally, Completely Not-Creepy Chimney Sweep** will not find an excuse to "check something with the chimney upstairs," slip into your bedroom, slowly open the dresser drawer next to your bed, and look for something naughty that will give him days of material for self-pleasuring. He will not go to his buddies back at **Totally, Completely Not-Creepy Chimney Sweep** headquarters and say, "You need to get a load of the rack on that lady down on Milford Street." And it should go without saying that your **Totally, Completely Not-Creepy Chimney Sweep** will not then look you up on the Internet and try to friend you on Facebook or follow you on Twitter.

That will never happen. Why? Because we are not men. We are *professionals.* Wear that thong all you want, we're not looking! Trust in us, and we'll treat your chimney like the Queen you are. Call us today!

◆

Dad Confirms Child's Worst Fears in Life

Suburgatory, USA—A dad who works as an actuary can't resist ghoulishly confirming his child's worst fears in life, in what's been described as perhaps the worst bedtime tuck-in talk ever captured on video.

Joe Gardner's wife Cherie surreptitiously recorded the incident with the couple's ten-year-old son, Andrew, and is about to post it on YouTube.

"Why would I put this horror show with the two people I love most in the world up for all to see? I'll tell you why. Joe is the greatest, most wonderful dad, but he doesn't believe me when I tell him that he is surely scaring the living shit out of our child, not to mention destroying his dreams and ambitions. And I need the rest of the world to tell him he's out of his mind and needs to stop," said Cherie.

Joe tried to defend himself. "What can I say? I've always had a weird talent for doom even as a child. Lady Gaga's right: I was born this way. I'm not ashamed! Then when I kicked ass in math, well, doom + math = boom! I'm an actuary! I love my job and yes, I do want my kid to know what disasters he really has to fear in life and what he doesn't."

"But honey, you're also a *dad*, and you should be saying to him, these terrible things will *never happen*," Cherie said.

"Actuaries never say never. You should know that by now, Cherie," Joe responded.

Exasperated, Cherie loaded the YouTube clip and played it. Then she pointed her finger at this reporter. "*You* tell me how crazy this is."

Joe: *Bedtime, Polar Bear [Andrew's nickname]! How was your day?*

Andrew: *Great, Dad! We did a unit on space in school. It was soooo cool; I think I want to be an astronaut. My teacher thought that was great.*

Joe: *Well, it's a really cool field that's for sure, but you should know the odds of becoming an astronaut are 13,000,200 to 1. The odds are better at becoming President. But you know, that's a real long shot, too. That's 10 million to 1! Probably better to think a little more practically about things to do with your life.*

Andrew: *Oh.*

Joe: *Hey, Mom said you looked a little freaked when that thunderstorm came through this afternoon.*

Andrew: *Well . . . a little.*

Joe: *Listen, Polar Bear. Daddy knows more than anyone about whether you should worry—it's what I do all day long at work. I'll tell you whether you really have to worry a lot about lightning. Compared to other stuff that can kill you, the answer is no. I mean, you have a way way higher chance of dying in the car on the way to school! Or in the bathtub right there [pointing to the bathroom]! And not by drowning, but by falling; so try to keep your feet steady in there, buddy! Ha ha ha. Heck, even the lawnmower's way more deadly than lightning. You know what's weird?*

Andrew: *What, Dad?*

Joe: *You'd* think *your risk of dying by chainsaw would be higher than dying by the lawnmower but, well, you'd be wrong—lawnmower wins! Maybe we shouldn't talk about all this.*

Andrew: *No, tell me, Daddy.*

Joe: *Well you always hear that the most dangerous thing you do is get in the car every day and that's true, no doubt about it. But while the chances are very high that you will be in an accident at some point, the chances you'll* die *in that accident are pretty low. Lower, in fact, than the chances of being murdered! Lower even than the chances that a catastrophic asteroid will hit the Earth! Which sounds crazy, but boy when you crunch the numbers, it doesn't start looking so unlikely. Those big scary Hollywood movies? Well, they may not be so far off.*

Within just a half hour of the YouTube clip being up, comments began to appear: "Douchebag." "You are one sick and scary bastard." "So, I can't get pregnant and this psycho gets to be a parent?" "Paging protective services!"

With that last comment, Cherie quickly took the clip down, but not before saying to Joe, accusingly, "You see?????" Joe, looking deflated, said he would go check in on Andrew to see if he was OK.

Joe: *Bear, I'm so sorry for our little talk tonight. So, so sorry.*

Andrew: *Why, Daddy?*

Joe: *Well I guess I sort of told you to forget about being an astronaut and then I talked about all that awful stuff that can happen.*

Andrew: *It's OK, Dad! I wasn't scared at all. I thought it was so cool! I can't wait to tell the boys all that cool stuff at school!* Especially *that death by chainsaw part!*

Joe: *Well, don't scare them too much. And you can be an astronaut if you want to be. You're my best boy. You can be anything you want to be.*

Andrew: *I don't want to be an astronaut anymore. Dad?*

Joe: *Yes, Andrew?*

Andrew: *What are my chances of becoming an actuary?*

In a flash, Joe went from looking chastened to elated. He gave Andrew a bear hug and said, "Chances are sky-high."

◆

SHOUT OUT

Message to Husband: Stop Getting Boners When I Cook

Beatrice Mathers is a mom and corporate lawyer who lives on Thomas Street.

I take to the Shout Out today, as a proud feminist married to a husband who I *thought* was a proud feminist, too. Except now the only time—and I'm not exaggerating—the *only* time he gets a boner for me is when I'm in the kitchen.

When I was a girl, I remember watching the classic '70s horror movie *The Stepford Wives,* and being disgusted that the men were massively turned on by the fantastic cooking of the sexy domestic robots they had created. "She cooks as good as she looks" is the line I remember best.

But I don't have one of those suburban body-snatcher husbands, right? Or do I? My husband Bill is my own private Dennis Kucinich. Most of his friends are women, half of which are lesbians, and there is the guy from high school who got a sex change but still likes women so she's now a lesbian, too. All are welcomed in the warm embrace of our anything-goes, super-liberal home. We've been together for nearly twenty years but didn't get married until I was eight months pregnant, and when we did it was at the Justice of the Peace and I wore a stained chambray maternity jumper (gay men everywhere are weeping at this). My husband got really sad when feminist Bella Abzug died, cried during the Harvey Milk movie, and once told me he didn't care if I ever shaved.

And yet as soon as our son was safely swaddled in our first suburban home, he seemed to forget that I used a microwave almost exclusively when we lived together for the three or so meals a week I ate at home. Back then, "cooking" meant using the stove top to boil water. Now, I quickly saw that it was here, in the kitchen, that he was most attracted to me. Those times when he remembered when I was a real professional kicking ass on the job? Oh, that's nice, honey. But put me in front of the stove endlessly stirring some chocolate pudding? Watch out, Daddy's zooming in like a predator drone to sex me up! "Woman, why don't you go in the kitchen and make me a sandwich." That was now my life, not a joke. (OK, apology break here to Bill for serving up my own steaming pile of hyperbole. He would never, ever say that to me, and not because I would lacerate his genitals, which I *would*, but because he's not a caveman. That said, you can damn well bet that he'd still love that sandwich, and love me a little more because I made it for him.)

The problem for wives, of course, is that a woman who achieves at work can be an absolute flop at homemaking. Not me, of course (cough, splutter). And we are often blindsided, left to wonder if we really knew our husbands and whether they ever valued us for what we are truly good at: Working in a goddamn office, dumbass! What do you think I went to an Ivy League school for? To flip your fucking pancakes? The fact that it isn't intentional makes it even more insidious, as if even an enlightened man like my own can't resist the siren song of sexist expectations. Bill said it feels completely natural and instinctual that he has this attraction to my domestic side. Yeah, well, my talents in the domestic arts feel about as natural to me as a pair of silicone double-Ds. Oops, gotta go, almost dinnertime. Now, let's see, was that bean burrito supposed to be nuked for a minute thirty or two minutes?

◆

Asperger's Dad Unlikely
Sex Symbol at School Pickup

Suburgatory, USA—A dad with undiagnosed Asperger's syndrome has become an unlikely sex symbol for the moms in the Walker School pickup line, because of his candor, weight-lifting regimen, and "special interest" that is unusually appropriate for socializing with other moms.

"How do we know he has Asperger's?" said Lindsay Cooper. "Gee, I don't know, maybe because these days every one of us either knows a kid with Asperger's or has one ourselves? Trust me. We know it when we see it. And with Mark, we like what we see."

Mark Toomey works from home as a computer programmer and so is more available than his wife to pick up their children from school.

Beth Barton describes him this way:

"He's hot, he's blunt, he's emotionally unavailable, and, well that's like a triple whammy turn-on. Oh, and you heard about his awesome 'special interest,' right? And don't forget those rock-hard abs," said Barton.

Part of Toomey's never-changing routine is intensive weight-lifting. "Ladies, guess who was at the pond last week. Oh. My. God," said Melissa Bandar to the other moms, while smiling and nodding. They joined her, smiling and nodding.

But the ladies say his looks come second to his "thrilling" and "provocative" honesty. Bandar said, "One time he walked right up to me, while I was talking to someone else, and he just blurted out, 'You have the most beautiful breasts.' Then he immediately looked worried, and I wanted to touch him on the arm, but you know, I know he flinches a bit, so I held back. He was so cute. He said, 'I'm sorry, I don't have much of a filter, do other people tell you that you have beautiful breasts?' I said, 'Not enough of them, honey!'"

Geri McGovern had her own sizzling encounter.

"One time I was sitting next to him while waiting for Carter to get out of physical therapy. We were talking about our pasts and he just abruptly launched into this little speech about puberty: 'Do you remember when you were a teenager and you just had that surge of sexual hormones, and you could just feel that sexual drive coursing through your veins, pump pump pump, like you didn't really know what you needed but whatever it was you really really needed it?' By the time he was done, oh God, I was seriously breathless."

His candor and unusual talent for detail and memory also make him an incorrigible gossip, which the moms love. Said Bandar, "He'll always remember which parent was shit-faced at the school benefit or the time he noticed that Gina's skirt had changed between drop-off and pickup and the whiff of cologne on her, which he said he knew was Karl Wagner's [not Gina's husband]. He's like the Sherlock Holmes of gossip!"

But McGovern doesn't think he's a gossip, exactly. "You know I was thinking about it and he's not really a gossip because to be a gossip you have to *know* you're not supposed to say something, and say it anyway. But Mark, he doesn't know he's supposed to zip a lip. So he's totally blameless shoveling all that great dirt at us. And we lap it up."

But perhaps Toomey's most unlikely selling point involves his "special interest," which is an obsession with a single topic: Oprah Winfrey. While Winfrey's show has ended, she is still a subject of fascination to the moms at pickup, who grew up watching her.

"He's like a walking Oprah bible. He can tell you what the audience got at the "Favorite Things" episode—every single year they did it. He knows every detail behind the Tom Cruise couch-jumping thing. But the best is that he has a *spreadsheet* that tracks public records and the fates of everyone who has ever appeared on the show. So you want to know whatever happened to that horrible crackhead mother or the Klansman who came out as gay, he might just have it. Oprah shoulda hired that guy," said McGovern.

While Toomey will tell you anything you want about Oprah, he is not forthcoming emotionally, which is typical for many with Asperger's. This hasn't deterred the moms.

"Oh, no way! He maintains the mystery," Bandar said. "You know," she added, "he has a lot of trouble, no surprise, with eye contact. But when he *does* make eye contact? It's like a few seconds of pure magic."

And what does Toomey say about all this? He shifted a bit uncomfortably and didn't look this reporter in the eyes, but said, "I haven't had it so easy my whole life making friends. My wife saved my life but next to her, these moms are the best things that ever happened to me. Well, them and Oprah."

◆

Woman with Eating Disorder Considers Meth

Suburgatory, USA—A church drug-awareness program has backfired in spectacular fashion for a mom who has long battled an eating disorder.

Janet Gosling attended a session on drug addiction in the community, which included a harrowing anti-drug photo collection called "Faces of Meth." It shows in frightening detail the physical toll that meth abuse takes on a body, tracking mug shots from habitual users over time.

"Now, ladies and gentlemen," said session leader and police officer Bill Barry, clicking through the befores and afters. "As you can see, meth simply ravages people who once had bright futures and leaves them diminished and often deformed." There were audible gasps in the room.

Gosling was one of those gasping, but not for the reasons Barry intended. Gosling has long wrestled with an eating disorder and body image dysmorphia, which she actually considers a "gift" from what she calls "thin God." Janet sat with her friend Debbie Flander.

Debbie: *Oh my God. Nasty.*

Janet: *Right . . . yeah . . . wow. Um . . . but . . . look how thin that one got.*

Debbie: *But Janet, she has sores covering her face. Oozing sores.*

Janet: *Oh yeah, I guess that's bad but you know, there's always a product for that. Try laxatives and see what that does to you— that stuff is poison. Works like you wouldn't believe, but you end up dribbling poop uncontrollably. This cop should be talking about that stuff.*

Barry clicked on the "before" image of another abuser.

Janet: *Look at that fatty! She musta been 135 pounds. No wonder she felt the need to abuse drugs.*

Debbie put her hand to her forehead as Barry clicked on the "after."

Janet: *Now look at that. See, she's totally normal now.*

Debbie: *Janet, she looks like a zombie ghoul about to come and scoop out your brains for breakfast.*

Janet: *Oh, I think these people are so amazingly high that they don't even remember what breakfast is. Imagine that.*

Barry described the woman's fate. "This abuser lit her trailer on fire when her home meth lab exploded. She lost everything."

Janet: *Well, at least she can go buy some new "thin" clothes! Debbie, stop it, I'm just kidding! I mean, sort of?*

Barry chose a final woman to illustrate meth's degrading effects. She now suffers from so-called "Meth Mouth," in which the constant use of meth causes catastrophic effects to the oral cavity.

Janet: *Look at how sculpted her face is now! She started out looking like Rosie O'Donnell and now she looks like a thinner Maria Shriver! So dramatic.*

Debbie: *Yeah Janet, a toothless, wild-eyed, sore-scratching Maria Shriver.*

Janet: *You know, bulimia rots your teeth, too. It gives you horrific breath and burns up your GI lining. We all pick our battles in this life.*

As the presentation ended, Janet went up to thank Officer Barry for his outreach and said, "Which parts of town are known for selling meth? I . . . I . . . really want to make sure I keep my kid away from those places."

Status Wrappers, Inc.

Ever felt the shame of being caught carrying . . . a Wal-Mart shopping bag? Or being spotted feeding your beloved children non-organic crap that they love, and you love as well? Does that cute new sweater really seem that cute when people see it sitting there in a bag from Kohl's?

At **Status Wrappers** we provide you with the cover you need to tote around your purchases without embarrassment. Whether it's the spanking new Nordstrom bag or the well-worn, but current issue of the *New Yorker,* which *of course* you read cover to cover (Wink, Wink!), or the wide selection of Annie's Organic boxes, we will provide you with the perfect receptacle to house or hide the crap products you really love, without the slightly raised eyebrow or snippy behind-the-back comment.

Here's a testimonial from one satisfied customer:

"One day I had a stack, and I'm not lying, a *stack* of flattened McDonald's Happy Meal boxes sitting in my passenger's seat when I saw that totally snotty bitch from my daughter's ballet class walking toward my car. I was immediately able to cover the stack with both a copy of *Vanity Fair* and a Whole Foods reusable tote with three boxes of Earth's Best Elmo's Pasta with Sauce with Carrots and Broccoli. Thank you, thank you, Status Wrappers!"

You know what your parents always told you? Don't judge a book by its cover? Well, you know now, that was a load of shit! Everyone judges a book by its cover. Welcome to adulthood! So what's that cover going to be? Let **Status Wrappers** be *your* cover, in a judge-or-be-judged world!

◆

Dad Pretends IKEA Is
Child Cultural Enrichment

Suburgatory, USA—A local dad was outed for pretending IKEA was a culturally enriching outing for his son.

Peter Marello lost his job eight months ago and is now the primary care provider for his four-year-old son James Patrick. Marello admits to being "kinda lost" and one day, on a quest to find a garlic press, he made his first-ever visit to IKEA. He found a lot more than he bargained for. "They have free childcare, food that doesn't break the five-dollar mark, clean bathrooms, and nice people. And of course, modern Swedish design at quality prices. Life's just a lot brighter and shinier at IKEA."

How did his regular IKEA pilgrimages begin?

"It sort of evolved . . . how I started going so much." Marello said sheepishly. "At first, I made a list of those little odds and ends you need but never buy—the new silverware tray, new knobs for the bathroom, new curtain rod—but then I just bagged the list and said, 'Fuck it.'"

Now they go a few times a week, with Marello dropping James Patrick in "Småland," IKEA's free child-care drop-off and what James Patrick actually thinks IKEA is called. Then Marello finds a comfortable spot in the store's vast cafeteria and sits down with his bottomless coffee and iPad. If no children are there, he switches the TV channel to ESPN to catch up on the scores; a few IKEA associates usually join him for that.

When James Patrick's child-care hour is up, Marello retrieves him and they visit parts of the store that James Patrick has named: the "Land of a Thousand Bedrooms" and "Magical Forest," where they play hide and seek among the artificial plants. They finish their visit with a cinnamon bun and a quick chat with Stephen Marsden in Returns and Exchanges, who especially loves James Patrick because his own grandchild lives hours away. "Sometimes if my wife works late we go for Wednesday Rib Night—it is off the wall cheap and James Patrick loves the Swedish meatballs," said Marello.

But he doesn't tell his wife, Jill, a busy corporate executive, where they go for ribs. Instead of admitting that he and James Patrick have unofficially joined the IKEA family, he tries to avoid detailing their outings, or, when pressed, says that they were attending a "museum of Scandinavian design and culture." Then James Patrick adds, "It's called Småland."

Marello was outed, however, while at the home of friends Marisa and Joe Mucha, empty nesters Marello used to work with. While catching up, they asked Marello what he and James Patrick do together during the day and James Patrick immediately said "Smaaalannd!" Marello quickly described Småland as a "small museum with a focus on Scandinavian design and culture," and hoped that would be the end of it. "Wow, Scandinavian design and culture? That sounds totally random, but these days I guess there's a museum for everything," said Marisa.

James Patrick said, "It's not small, Daddy, it's huge. You should see the furniture pickup area!"

Joe asked, "What did you say, James Patrick?"

Marello said, "Oh he's just talking about a part of the museum where you can touch the furniture. So what else is going on with you guys?"

Marisa, already looking suspicious asked James Patrick, "Sooooo, what else do you do at the museum of Scandinavian design and culture?"

"Oh, eat cinnamon buns and jump into the huge ball pit and throw balls all over and go to the Land of a Thousand Bedrooms and we talk to Stephen and . . . hey," James Patrick said, running his hands up and down the living room chair. "This is the Ektorp Jennylund!"

At this point, the jig was up, and while Marello looked mortified, Joe said, "James Patrick, does the museum of Scandinavian design and culture have a big sign with the letters I K E A?"

"Yes! Does that spell Smaaaland?"

Marello's friends erupted in riotous laughter and asked why he didn't just say he was going to IKEA. "It sounds pathetic! And don't you dare tell Jill, I don't know how, but she still hasn't figured it out. She's totally turned into a man now, and barely even asks about our day. But she'd still kill me if she found out I wasn't providing James Patrick with 'enrichment.'"

Joe Mucha said, "Oh, don't beat yourself up. When you're a parent you gotta do what you gotta do to just get through it. Don't make yourself crazy. We know all about that, right Maris?"

Marisa agreed. "James Patrick enjoys it, you enjoy it. End of story."

Not quite. James Patrick emerged from the kitchen with a melon baller.

"This toy is miscontinued."

"*Dis*continued, James Patrick," Marello said.

"But you can bring it back and get store credit—ask for Stephen and tell him James Patrick said Hi!"

◆

Mom's Thrill Dashed by
Sex and the City's Miranda

Suburgatory, USA—A mom tried to appear blasé—and failed—about news that actress Cynthia Nixon has not only moved to town, but has also enrolled her child at the local school.

"Oh yeah, it's a great school that we're zoned for. We've really lucked out. Oh and you know, I think Cynthia Nixon's new in town and she's zoned for the school, too," said Joyce Birney, in an intentionally offhanded way en route to the first day of classes for her nine-year-old, Aaron.

Arriving at the school, Birney said, "Yeah I mean we could have easily afforded to send Aaron to Briarcliff, but we just thought, we have a great school right here, people love it, and—*Holy shit, there's Miranda!* I mean, um, there's Cynthia Nixon."

Birney's husband, Robert, turned away quickly. "I don't know how I'm going to talk to her when I know what her boobs look like the whole time. They're little and super white, not my bag. I mean, not *bad* or anything, any boobs are better than no boobs at all, but, I don't know, it's going to be distracting to me."

Nixon had arrived with her partner, public education activist Christine Marinoni. As Birney and her husband attempted to hide their furtive glances, Birney discussed the values that she believes she shares with Cynthia Nixon. "You know, Miranda, she realized you have to give up your 'city dream' eventually. Leave Manhattan. Try Brooklyn. Now she's here. Just like me! Can't send your kids to those crap schools in the city. She was always the most sensible of the four girls. Oh, and she's a lawyer, too, who didn't stop working after Brady came along. Oh, there's Aaron's teacher. We need to talk to her, I guess."

The teacher was already speaking with Marinoni, as Birney waited her turn. "Cynthia must really respect her. She *never* respected Steve. Now this relationship must be built on something real and lasting. That woman must worship Miranda!"

As Marinoni finished, Birney whispered to her husband, "Let's blow off the teacher," and decided it was "too much of a coincidence not to say hello" to Nixon, the coincidence being "She's just a mom like I am."

Birney introduced herself to Nixon and said, "We're thrilled that you've moved to town! It'll take some getting used to life outside the big city and all but it's worth it for the kids, right?!"

Nixon very cordially said, "It's lovely to meet you! But we are only in town for six months."

Birney looked crestfallen. "So you didn't move here—move here?" Nixon said no. Birney then brightened, "Wait, you're not shooting the next *Sex and the City* movie out here, are you????"

"Oh no no! I'm doing the play *Angels in America* at the McClaren." Nixon said.

"Wow, that must be such a drag for you after shooting with all that glamour and fun costumes in Abu Dhabi!" said Birney, in what her husband Robert calls her "annoying girl-talk tone."

"Actually that was shot in Morocco. And I'm not knocking *Sex and the City* at all, but really theater is my first love, so it's a thrill for me to be here, even though we are heartbroken to take the kids out of P.S. 34 back in the city—it's . . . um . . ." Nixon looked around. "It's a little more diverse. And in a way, this is really a lot more like what you'd find in private school. Christine and I really believe in diverse public education. I'm sure it's great here though!" said Nixon, seemingly trying to soften the blow.

"Ah well, great to meet you," Birney said. As they walked away, Birney looked deflated, and whispered to Robert, "Such a boring snotty lesbian."

◆

The Calorie-Schmalorie Pizza Kitchen

Boy, there's no bigger buzzkill than eating that enormous bacon cheese hamburger with fried onions and fried egg and then stumbling upon that nasty nutritional information. We know what it feels like: Oh My Fucking God. I just ate in one meal what a whole African village might get in a day!

Well, at **The Calorie-Schmalorie Pizza Kitchen** we will never, ever reveal the calories in our delectable dishes. To anyone. What if we're forced by the arm of the law to post our calories? Then we'll just pack it in; that's how important our commitment to ignorance in eating is.

Not only will we avoid public posting and online customizable calculators, but we will resist all direct questions from our patrons. Let's say you're thinking of eating our wonderful, decadent Death by Chocolate Molten Lava Cake, and you think, "Gee, I should ask the waiter the nutritional content of that Lava Cake even though I really, really don't want to." Finally you cave and ask. Our waiters will simply tell you, "You look so thin! Do you work out? You must really deserve our wonderful cake, because you are really taking care of yourself." Don't try to persist. Our waiters are trained to withstand al-Qaeda terrorist interrogation—they're not going to spill our secrets to little ole pesky (and thin) you!

Worry about your ass somewhere else. Eat, enjoy, and don't look back. **The Calorie-Schmalorie Pizza Kitchen.**

❖

Feared Room Mommies Divide Iraqi Oil Revenue

Suburgatory, USA—The Room Mommies, infamous for their take-no-prisoners negotiating tactics, have been dispatched to settle an issue that's dogged Iraq in the years since the 2003 US invasion: the division of oil revenue among rival factions.

Mommies Christina Hohn, Rachel Tovacs, and Lisa Epstein traveled with military escort to Baghdad, at the behest of Iraqi president Jalal Talabani. Hohn spoke from inside the still heavily fortified Green Zone.

"Listen, last year when we had to manage the holiday gifts at the preschool and divide them between the teachers, it was just a major, massive shit storm. Every teacher is supposed to get the same amount, the float teachers get a little less, Bernardo the facilities guy, he gets some too. And what happens? We have to drag these mothers kicking and screaming out of Starbucks to cough up the cash. And do they accept our authority?"

Epstein, as is custom among the Room Mommies, finished Hohn's thought for her.

". . . NO! One parent went renegade and snuck in some big Neiman card on the sly. One bought organic food baskets with kombucha or some bullshit granola crap. Some gave nothing, but still wanted their kid's handprint on the group card. The Bible thumper gave her own card with a creepy hologram Jesus, you know, like, right out of *Carrie*, and then gives it to Miss Levine. *LUH-vine!* One actually gave swag from work. . . ."

Mommy Tovacs grabbed the microphone from Epstein and tried to shout over the din of mortar fire.

". . . then the teacher who got swag is pissed at the teacher who got the Neiman gift card. The teacher who got kombucha had no clue what it was. Then Miss Levine filed a complaint about the Jesus card. But you know what? We got them to take their junk back and give us cash, talked Levine off the ledge, and handed out perfectly apportioned Amex gift cards, all before holiday break. And we're going to get the dirty work done here in Baghdad, too. The Kurds, the Shia, and the Sunnis, they know our rep. We're not here to make friends. We're gonna knock some heads before bath and bedtime, and everyone will get their fair share of those oil dollars."

After the morning's first meeting, which featured a nutrient-dense snack and water sippy cups, Mommy Tovacs was ebullient at their progress. "Now, look, with 59 percent of Iraq's oil reserves concentrated in southern Basra we pointed out to the Shia that poor Dahook, Anbar, Babel, and Dewaniya have nothing! Is that fair to Dahook, Anbar, Babel, and Dewaniya? No! And the Shia said politely, 'No, Mommy Tovacs.'"

Epstein said this to the Kurds. "I know, I know the Sunnis did the gassing and all, but being good friends means forgiving. And sharing. And with 12 percent of total reserves held in Kurd-controlled Kirkuk, you have to share. You *must* share."

The Kurdish representative, however, was visibly shaken by what happened behind closed doors. "Saddam . . . we praise Allah and the George Bush for saving us from that pure evil set upon our land. But these ladies, uhhhh, Saddam never met these ladies. Saddam, filthy dog, he terrified me. And the Sunnis, those puppies of the filthy dog, they scare me. But not like this. Now I see that I need to work on my sharing. I *will* work on my sharing."

The Shia cleric, who demanded that the Room Mommies wear the hijab head cover during the talks, was similarly rattled by the morning's brinkmanship. "I thought, well, I mean, I thought the hijab would soften the Room Mommies, but it didn't work. These ladies . . . well . . . I've faced fedayeen [torture squads] who'll give you cigarettes and sweets. And mercy."

The Sunni negotiator, a former Baath party member and accused war criminal, was more blunt. "We'll do whatever the Room Mommies tell us and, *inshallah*, they'll go home, they'll take those terrible devices—the nasal aspirator and the anal thermometer—away, and we can, what did that Jew lady call it? 'Go nappy.'"

◆

Waitress Wages Anti-Foodie
Jihad on Chowhound

Suburgatory, USA—A local woman, fed up with the high-end restaurant where she waitresses and the people who eat there, has launched an anonymous online jihad on the foodie website Chowhound.

"OK, [head chef] Graydon would be *horror-fied* that you are calling it 'high-end.' Because that sounds fancy and contrived, which, of course, Ploughshare isn't at all. It's just farm-to-table pure authenticity on a plate! This shit will set you back two hundred bucks for one dinner; the most expensive food in suburbia within a hundred miles, but it doesn't matter. It's still 'rustic comfort food,' isn't it? Whatever that means."

The woman spoke to this reporter at the Elm Street Applebee's. She asked to remain anonymous, and would like to be referred to by the Internet name she uses while terrorizing the unsuspecting foodies on the section of Chowhound devoted to the region. Her Internet name is EatMyShit.

EatMyShit feels like it is her responsibility to puncture the illusions and pretensions of the foodies who make her job torture.

"So go to Ploughshare and look at the communal tables with that tiny hint of dust. That is *not* naturally occurring dust. It's *artfully dusted every morning.* Do you know that the maple used for those tables is recovered wood from a 1950s bowling alley? Because you know what foodies also like when they're not eating food that's farm-to-table? Irony! Mmmmm mmmm yummy yummy, gobble gobble, gimme my lobster gruyere mac and cheese and a Pabst Blue Ribbon, please!"

EatMyShit realized she could take out her many frustrations on the foodie website Chowhound, and away she went.

"Loco-More" asked if anyone knew where he could find regionally sourced wild ramps. EatMyShit responded: "You mean you need a bag of onions? Yes, Wal-Mart has started selling produce. Local enough for you? And does every fucking ingredient have to have a zip code attached to it?"

"Chowdah-hound" was in search of the perfect Tunisian Mahdjouba Djazairia sandwich with "round, flat griddled bread." EatMyShit wrote, "Did you hear that a poor Tunisian man selling vegetables from a pushcart set himself on fire and touched off a revolution that swept the Middle East? No? Oh right, you're too busy chasing down your super-special-ethnic-I'm-the-coolest-sandwich."

EatMyShit's favorite guerrilla tactic is searching for people who use the words "famished" or "starved" or "dying" for something like, say, white truffle oil or nettle soup, and then posting pictures of emaciated Somali children in response.

Just where did this seemingly bottomless pit of anger come from? "You know, it's not really that fun serving food you yourself can't afford. I'd almost rather work in a place that actually screams out that it's high-end, instead of pretending to be so simple and virtuous. Then you see these people trying to seem so casual snapping pictures of their precious dinners and putting it on Facebook like they just won the fucking Nobel Peace Prize for Eating."

So when "Gordough" asked on Chowhound about the ambiance at Ploughshare, EatMyShit was eager to respond: "Douchebag with a side of Hipster. Oh, and you know the only thing worse than a hipster? An old, gray-haired *suburban* hipster. Give it the fuck up already."

"Yeah, so I guess I have a really strong position on this topic and . . . and . . ." EatMyShit unexpectedly started tearing up. "Well, to be really honest, my boyfriend Graydon—he's the chef at Ploughshare. He broke up with me last month. Maybe it's made me a little crazy. . . . Love sucks, doesn't it? Miss?" she said to the Applebee's waitress. "Can I get the Bloomin' Onion?"

◆

SHOUT OUT

The House that Ate My Husband

Carla Baker is a wife and mother who lives on Linden Street.

I take to the Shout Out section today to deliver a cautionary tale to my fellow wives out there.

It was July 16, 2007. Yes I remember the exact date, how could I not? How can a loving wife and mother erase from her mind that horrible day when her family was ripped away from her without warning? The day I signed my name on all those dotted lines, page after page, thinking I was forging a bright future for my son, my husband, and me, too, in our new suburban town. But that wasn't how it all worked out. No, no it did not.

It was the moment Steve was stolen from me by a mistress who consumes his heart, his time, his very soul. She is unrelenting in her demands, and her steely grip on him is complete. To add insult to injury, while I can still rock a size 8 on a thin day, she is built like a brick house. Because she is a brick house. Our house. And I curse the day I let that fat bitch into my life.

As soon as he saw her, when that old-hag broker pimped her out to us, he had to have her. His hand ran gently across her mantle. He traced the curves of her countertops. It was only then that I realized that I hadn't seen Steve look like this in years: He looked happy. I could tell that this was it, it was her or nothing. I thought she was borderline white trash, I mean, her kitchen? Those tacky cabinets? Steve insisted we could class her up. She just needed our help. Steve really meant *his* help, his tender, knowing touch. And within weeks of that day we closed, as the tools piled up and the projects got their own Excel spreadsheet, I knew he was hooked. He was already out the door emotionally, and he was taking my preschool son with him.

She makes Steve feel needed in ways I never could. "Steeeve, my gutters are so clogged. Can you clean them out? Pleeeeze?" And he's out there in a flash. Sometimes he'll try to duck out and I'll catch him and demand to know where he's going. He can't look me in the eye or say it, but I know where he's headed: Home Depot. Because she loves sending him out on a whim, hoping he'll come back with some bauble to make her prettier. Whore-red paint for her shutters. A gaudy spotlight to show off her shapely front door. Anything to tart her up, to keep him coming back for more. And when he's not hanging off some part of her, I can see him drift, get that glazed look. I know he's thinking about her, what he wants to do with her next and how fast he can start. Then there was that time she called during dinner.

"Steeeve, the acid rain is falling on me. I'm burning! Can you come and power wash me? It's stinging me! Ow!" I told him if she ever called during dinner again, I was out of there. He shot back at me, "You know, every guy in town is just like me. You act like I'm some criminal or something!" I said, "They are *not* just like you. They bring in plumbers, landscapers, and handymen so they don't get too attached. But you couldn't resist, could you?"

There's always drama with her. I've always been sensible, reliable, predictable, easy-peasy; now I see what Steve has always wanted: a train wreck. He can't get enough of the excitement, the challenge. "Oh, no! How did this happen? Steve, helllp! My basement just flooded and you need to clean me up *now!* The mold, it's coming!" Then, "I don't know how this could have happened but my furnace shut down and I'm getting soooo cold, Steve!"

You know, I think I could accept this betrayal from Steve; I get it, relationships change, mature, grow old, grow tired. We're both adults. But she's sucked our little boy into her sickening web, too. He follows Steve around with his little play toolbox, anxious to see what Dad's all hot and bothered about. When I ask him to make muffins with me, Jackson will say "No Mommy, I have to help Daddy wee-gwout the tiles in the baff-woom!" And I see Steve's example imprinting itself on my little boy. It's what Steve's dad did to him. And I look ahead at Jackson's future and think, it's what Jackson will do to his wife, too. We all know it's a cycle.

She's taken everything dear from me. But I'm trapped. I can't leave because then that cunt would win. And we're underwater on our mortgage. Because of her. That filthy, good-for nothing homewrecker.

◆

Parents Called "Bad Jews" for Rejecting Sleepaway Camp

Suburgatory, USA—An area Jewish family has been harassed online and in person by those in their community who are flabbergasted by the parents' decision not to send their seven-year-old son to sleepaway camp.

"I want my boy home this summer. These people will have to pry him from my cold, dead hands," said Lori Metzner.

"How do you like that," said Bari Weiss, whose daughter attends Hebrew school with Metzner's son, Josh.

"There she is, quoting Charlton Heston. People thought he was a Jew, too. Well, he wasn't. I'm starting to think Lori is less of a Jew than he was! Ben Hur would have sent his kid to sleepaway camp, you can be damn sure of that."

At first, friends and acquaintances of Lori and Jeremy Metzner were gentle with the couple, as they tried to process the idea of a Jewish child just aimlessly kicking a ball around at home all summer, completely bereft of other young Jews. Some asked them, delicately, "Is there something wrong with Josh—is he sick?"

But once word got out that Josh was *not* sick, the gloves came off. It was decided among the Highland Street Jews that an intervention was needed. Two parents, Roni Sussman and Lisa Scher, banged hard on the door without warning one night and barreled in, giving the Metzners no chance to keep them out.

Roni: *Lori, we are really, really concerned about Josh.*

Lori: *Why?*

Lisa: *How is he going to learn about his Jewish identity if he doesn't go to sleepaway camp?*

Jeremy: *Considering I never see either of you at temple even on high holidays, I'm starting to think your Jewish identity is sleepaway camp.*

Roni: *Think of our terrible past. Our people died in the Holocaust and would have wanted our kids to go to sleepaway camp.*

Jeremy: *They had sleepaway camp in Nazi Germany?*

Lori: *Wait, are you saying you think Holocaust victims would want me to put my child on a bus to be sent away to a camp out in the woods a hundred miles away?*

Roni: *Lori, that's not funny.*

Jeremy: *Good one, Lor!*

Lisa: *You two are letting Hitler win!*

Undeterred, Lisa and Roni put up a Facebook page called "Save Joshy's Summer" in hopes of putting pressure on the Metzners. The page encouraged people to post their favorite camp stories and it attracted a few thousand camp-crazed Jewish adults from all over the world.

It remained generally positive, that is, until the Metzners decided to have some fun with it. First, Lori posted this. "All I learned at Camp Shalom was how to give a blow job." Then Jeremy said they had changed their minds and decided to send Josh to camp, which got dozens of "Likes" within minutes. Then he posted which camp—it was Sunnyvale—a well-known high-end camp that caters exclusively to WASPs.

A few minutes later, as those dozens of people "Unliked" the post, Jeremy added "Psych!" One response to the Metzner's ruse was this: "Why don't you send him to the Gaza Strip Hamas training camp, because that's the only place that'd want you."

Did these attacks upset the Metzners? Jeremy Metzner snorted, and said, "No. We're tough Jews." And is Josh going to miss being around his Jewish brethren this summer? He said, "I'm going to be with my best and favorite Jews in the whole world," pointing to his mom and dad.

◆

Dr. Drama

"When life hands you a problem, let's make it more interesting!"

Dear Dr. Drama:
I know this is going to sound really awful but I recently dealt with a painful breakup with my husband, at the same time that my single mom friend says she found the love of her life. "He's great with the kids, he's great in bed, he's got a great job, you name it, he's The One." Meanwhile I'm stuck in this suburb that has only about five single mothers, tops, and I'm suddenly the saddest loser around. I can't deal with the resentment, and I feel like a terrible person for even feeling this way. Any advice?

—Jealous in Suburgatory

Dear Jealous:
Wait, you *feel bad? Your* friend *is the one who should feel bad,*
because if there's anything I've learned in my many decades on
this horrible rock we call Earth, it's this: Happy couples need to
shut the fuck up. Now if they are teenagers, I give them a pass. If
they're so unattractive that this is their first, crazy-making burst
of love, fine. But any average suburban person over the age of
thirty? If they haven't figured out how much pain their joy causes
99 percent of the rest of the world, well, they are about two baby
steps away from sociopath.

Don't feel bad, Jealous. Just be patient. That happy will be
gone by the time the snow flies and you and your friend will
be back together saying "shut the fuck up" to the next clueless
couple shmushing their eternal love in your face. Because we all
know eternal love has a shelf life shorter than the box of your
kids' Go-Gurts in the fridge.

◆

New Atheist Bigger Asshole than Old Catholic

Suburgatory, USA—In a stunning development, our community's so-called New Atheist has out-assholed the Old Catholic.

"Yes, I definitely didn't think this was possible," said Brian Marooney, who judged this afternoon's clash of assholes at the Community Comes Alive! town event.

"Those Old Catholics are the worst. They try to explain away pedophile priests. They defend that psycho scumbag Mel Gibson. But still, those New Atheists, man, what else do they do other than think up new dorky ways to call five billion people around the world morons?" said Marooney.

"New Atheists" are a relatively recent addition to town and the broader community of non-believers. They strike a militant tone compared to "old" atheists, on what they say are the evils of organized religion and belief in general. But in doing so, many, though not all, have adopted a sarcastic attack-dog method, with slogans like "WWJD = We Won. Jesus Died." and "Too Stupid to Understand Science? Try Religion."

And so the clash of assholes at Community Comes Alive! began with the New Atheist and the Old Catholic sitting side-by-side at adjacent booths, though not communicating.

"That boy needs a good haircut and a draft card," said Old Catholic Gerry O'Connor. "Dad, they don't have draft cards anymore," said son Bob O'Connor, who insists he's not an Old Catholic, just keeping an eye on his dad, "who wanders off sometimes." What does Bob O'Connor believe in? "I attend the Church of Don't-Give-a-Shit," he said.

Gerry O'Connor festooned his booth with photographs of mangled fetuses and featured pamphlet material on why radical homosexuality, not criminal pedophilia, was the cause of the priest abuse scandal. He began a discussion about how "a few poofs and queers and that Lady Gaga should go back into the closet and slam the door." O'Connor continued, "Not seen and not heard. Those poofs and queers made our wonderful priests look like monsters."

Judge Brian Marooney said, "Wow. That was really bad. The New Atheist is going to have to bring it."

Ethan Barthold, who has tattooed a New Atheist "A" on his arm, was ready for the challenge. "People who don't want their beliefs laughed at shouldn't have such funny beliefs.

We feel sorry for the theists, but my patience with their stupidity has come to an end. If they were capable of rational thought—and the jury's out on that one—then maybe they would see the evil that their feeble-minded delusions cause."

Barthold's booth had a banner touting "National Idiot Outreach Day," and it featured various ironic and sarcastic attacks on people of faith such as ATHEISTS—WINNING SINCE 33 AD; No GODS. No MULLETS; JESUS SAVES . . . YOU FROM THINKING FOR YOURSELF.

"Whoa, this is a really tough call," said Judge Marooney. "I mean, that Old Catholic really is hateful, but he is sort of sad, like, stuck in an Archie Bunker time warp. But that New Atheist, I mean, he's just a complete asshat. So I'm going to say, after careful thought, that the New Atheist has out-assholed the Old Catholic."

Marooney did say to take his judgment with a grain of salt. "I'm an atheist and I think people like Ethan are hurting the cause. If they spent half as much time doing charity outreach in the name of atheism as they did thinking up those ridiculous insults, and gotchas, then maybe we'd be getting somewhere. How do they think evangelicals took over half of Latin America? *Charity.* Part of me wants to be wrong about atheism just so I can see God smack that smirk off Barthold's face. Watching that dude be wrong for an eternity? I'm there. Oh my God, look!"

Marooney pointed at Barthold's sign, ATHEISTS—WINNING SINCE 33 AD, but realized Barthold had misspelled "Atheists" as "Athiests."

Marooney laughed hard and said, "A is for Awesome. *And* Asshole."

◆

Faith for a Day Seat Fillers

There's nothing more disheartening on your sacred day of worship than walking into your church or temple and finding the room where you commune with your savior nearly empty. God's in the room, no doubt, but where is everyone else? If you're thinking Dunkin' Donuts, you're probably right. They better hope there's Dunkin' Donuts in Hell!

The empty seats, the unmistakable whiff of dying faith. It's a pox on the soul of the congregation, and a self-fulfilling prophecy: Empty seats beget empty seats until one day, the temple board or the diocese calls and Father Murphy or Rabbi Moshe is knocking hard on the door of God's welfare office. So what's a priest, reverend, or rabbi to do?

Introducing **Faith for a Day Seat Fillers**, where for a small per-person fee, young and vibrant church- and temple-goers will enthusiastically attend your services. They will be trained in the specific faith, but cannot directly be asked any questions beyond what is found in Wikipedia.

So take action. Take just a little out of that dwindling pass-the-basket pocket change from those Grandmas and Grandpas still turning out week after week, God bless 'em. Turn that mother out, and pack that place to the rafters, with **Faith for a Day Seat Fillers**. You know The Boss upstairs is watching and he's one tough bastard. Don't let God decide you're just not worth His effort.

◆

Mom Discovers
The Sociopath Next Door

Suburgatory, USA—After reading the book *The Sociopath Next Door*, an area mom identified the sociopath, who is next door.

"It's Griffin! It's him in a nutshell, it's uncanny! I stayed up all night Googling everything you'd ever want to know about sociopaths!" said Mary Thibodeau.

The Sociopath Next Door by Martha Stout takes the idea of a sociopath—usually thought of as a violent criminal—and expands it to include the everyday deviant who might be "next door"—your coworker, college roommate, or in this case, an actual next-door neighbor, Griffin Driscoll. The popular book spawned an army of armchair psychologists diagnosing those around them, and Thibodeau is just the latest.

"So here's more sociopath, psychopath, and narcissist stuff I found on Google: *'Pecking order is extremely important to the sociopath. His outward appearance may be the picture of success with all the trappings of status aggressively and elaborately displayed. But his inner life is empty,'*" read Mary from her iPad.

"Well, that would explain 'The Rev,'" she said. That's what Mary and her husband Jim call Driscoll's habit of loudly revving his Porsche convertible each day in his driveway, a sound the Thibodeaus can only imagine is designed to attract attention to the expensive car.

"Yeah, well you *say* that annoys you, but you run out every time he does it just to look at that car," said Jim.

"Not true! It's because I can't believe how rude it is!" Mary said.

"So this stuff was on a support group for wives of every-day psychos," Mary continued. *"A sociopath will show little or no empathy and may lie to cover up his lack of feeling*—like the time that little girl from down the street got hurt on his property, and he did nothing and pretended he didn't see her even though I *saw* him strutting around half-dressed like a peacock on the deck."

"Yep," said Jim.

"The sociopath, while perhaps not violent to people, may use animals to satisfy his thirst for causing pain. Oh my God. The squirrel. Do you really think?" said Mary.

Mary Thibodeau was referring to a squirrel found on their property border that had been mauled to death in a way that, to Jim, looked highly unnatural.

"OK let me finish this paragraph from the support group: *A sociopath is often highly sexually appealing to . . .*" Mary abruptly stopped and turned red. Jim looked at her, grabbed the iPad, and finished ". . . *women!*" adding emphasis and drawing it out. *"The sociopath has a surface charm. And that can often be an aphrodisiac for women. Even to those who claim to find his behavior abhorrent."*

Jim put the iPad down triumphantly. "You're hot for the Sociopath Next Door. Nice! Maybe there are some cute serial killers in prison that you can start sending letters to! God, this is just like when you and every other thirty-some-thing housewife was obsessed with that psychotic killer Tony Soprano. What is *wrong* with you women? I mean, yeah, we men like big boobs and young girls but some of you freaks are attracted to men who might hurt you?"

"Leave my Tony out of it. He would *never* hurt an animal," Mary said.

◆

New Black Resident
Worst Racist in Town

Suburgatory, USA—A new black father who has joined our overwhelmingly white community is being described as the "worst racist in town."

Bradford Johnson described his family's move here very openly as a classic case of "white flight" from the section of the city where the population is 50 percent black or Hispanic and growing. This reporter thought using the term "white flight" was an unusual choice for a black person to use.

"Just because I'm black doesn't mean I give a rat's ass about other blacks. I want the same things white people do. To be far, far away from black people. To suggest that I love blacks just because I'm black, well, that's just racist."

Johnson has been wholeheartedly welcomed into his new affluent Westgate neighborhood, with residents appreciating the chance to have the appearance of diversity, even though Johnson's background makes him far more similar culturally to his neighbors than to the black or Hispanic server at the local Dunkin' Donuts. "The diversity I provide is that I am the first person *of any color* on our street to attend MIT."

Peggy Marist was thrilled at the idea of what she called "our own, personal Obamas!" Lowering her voice, Marist said, "They didn't seem black-black at all, and not even Michelle Obama–black. They're Barack-black all the way. Some of the kids bused in from the city are really black-black and kind of wild, so I was really excited for my Madison to have her own sweet 'Malia' to be friends with on the bus! We already have a gay, a bunch of Chinese all in one house, and even one Mexican. So the Johnsons seemed like the perfect

addition. But . . . well, Bradford has a little . . . anger. I think
he's, like, mad at America or something. I mean, not mad at
America but other black people." She had loudly whispered
the words "black people."

The white residents had a very clear idea of how their
interaction would be with Johnson: They would have light,
friendly contact in which his race would go unmentioned,
at all costs. But Johnson didn't comply. People would frequently say, "You must have really wanted your kids to enjoy
the great schools here!" He would be honest and reply, "Yes,
we wanted them away from those black people. Believe me,
you don't want your kids around them. If it's more than 10
percent black, well, I'd never send my kids there. They just
bring you down."

Johnson found himself very frustrated, and alienated
people with his blunt race-talk. "I thought they would want
to talk about black people as much as I do. Isn't that why I
moved here? Thank goodness I found Old Bill."

"Old Bill" Jesper, also known by his harsher critics as
"the Starbucks Klansman," now meets Bradford for coffee
a few days a week to discuss some of their favorite areas of
attack, like unwed mothers in the black community or the
evils of the drug trade. "They call *me* a racist? If I was a black
guy and got stuck in an alley, it's *Bradford* I'd worry about,
not poor old falling-apart Bill Jesper. I just like to rile people
up to pass the time. Johnson wants a race war. Him versus
the rest of 'hims.'"

Interestingly, Bradford has faced at least one moment of
true racism, but blames the incident on the failings of black
people. One time a new neighbor assumed that Bradford
was actually NFL player Deshaun Watson, one of the few

other prominent black residents in the area. The neighbor believed that the only way a black man could afford to live in the area was if he was a pro athlete. But rather than attack the neighbor for that assumption, Bradford blamed "the blacks." "That assumption is *not racist*. It's incontrovertible fact. There are not hardly enough rich black professionals and we have no one to blame but themselves."

So what does he make of the idea that he is viewed as the town's Obama? "I don't get that man. Obama had the perfect life, completely free from blacks, and then he picks up and moves to Chicago to be with all those, those people? But notice he didn't decide to stay in blackie-town. He had a plan to get out. And notice also," he said triumphantly, "did he send his girls to public school in D.C. to be with all those no-good blacks? Nope. Because he is a proud black man who wants the best for his black daughters, just like me."

◆

Macho Pottery Camp— Where Boys Become Men Who Become Potters

So your son wants to take up pottery. You're not worried he'll become gay. You're a modern man; gay is completely fine with you. What's *not* fine is the idea that you might be fostering a sensitive straight man. No one likes them!

At **Macho Pottery Camp,** we offer the full array of potter skills; but you won't walk in and find a gray-haired lady with a brocade vest and comfort clogs as your son's teacher. Oh no. Your pottery instructor is Marine Corps all the way, and the majority of them were honorably discharged. OOH-RAH! They will whip that clay into shape, just like they will your son. He'll "Semper Fire" a misshapen cup for Father's Day that says, "I love you Dad . . . for making me a man at **Macho Pottery Camp.**"

Also consider for your son our brother facility, **Macho Mime Camp.** That Invisible Box won't know what hit it when your badass son crushes it in a single imaginary blow! Call us now!

◆

Poor by Choice Meets Just Plain Poor

Suburgatory, USA—A woman who is poor by choice gave some less than helpful advice to a woman who is just plain poor, as the two of them were checking out groceries at the Bay Street Stop-n-Shop.

Kristin Perry lives in town and shops at the store regularly, as does Callie Bennett, who works there as a cashier and lives right outside the town line in the Edgemont trailer park. When Perry saw that Bennett had a food stamp swipe card, like she has, she thought she had found a kindred spirit. "Not too many poor people around here, we have to stick together!"

Perry attended Cornell University and then the Wharton Business School; her husband attended Dartmouth. Both grew up in an upper-middle-class suburb, and after college they both stepped on the upwardly-mobile work treadmill along with most of their peers. That is, until their first child was born.

"We just decided we wanted more out of life, and being poor was the answer. All that stuff we were accumulating and the time spent earning money to buy it was just making us emptier. Not everyone can handle the impoverished life, but for us it was the challenge of a lifetime, and we were eager to conquer it. With a small stipend from Mike's dad's stock dividends, I was able to leave my job and Mike was able to fulfill his dream of perfecting his craft." Which is? "His craft? I don't know, we keep our passions separate. You should ask him!"

Why did they choose to live in such an expensive town? "Of course, education is number one to us, so we were really lucky Mike's father supported our decision to be poor and bought us the house, which helped him on his taxes, too. Win-win!"

Store clerk Callie Bennett says she's just plain poor and comes from a long line of just plain poor people who came before her. With no chance to attend college, she feels lucky, though hardly pleased, to have her job at Stop-n-Shop. But, as it goes with the just plain poor, she is only just getting by, and has a new baby to boot. Bennett described her encounter with Perry.

"When I pulled out my EBT [food stamp] card, the scary hippie lady behind me sort of waved hers at me, with a small smile, like it was sign language for 'I'm poor, too, let's be friends!' Ugh I was so zonked from work, I just wanted to go the fuck *home*."

Perry noticed Bennett's several boxes of diapers. "Knowing that many other poor women don't know about the value of cloth-diapering to both the environment and their budgets, I thought maybe I would do some outreach." So she said, "Have you considered cloth diapers for your baby? It's soft on their bottoms, good for the globe, and it's practically free, and free's good for poor women like us, right?"

Bennett for a second just stared. Then she responded: "It's only free if you don't put any value on my time, and my time is worth fifteen bucks an hour, and I need every dollar from every hour and every minute that I work. You think I want to add disgusting 'cloth' diapers to my insane laundry load?"

Perry seemed chastened and said, "Well, it's really not that hard. You boil them, using tongs, about six times for about fifteen minutes to make them more absorbent and then you . . . "

Bennett looked at her, slack-jawed. "Why don't you worry about your own life and your own baby's bottom and your own boiled shit and I'll worry about mine? I have to think about my future and I *don't* plan to be poor forever." Bennett assumed, correctly, that Perry doesn't work. "Maybe if you got a *job*, you could dream bigger, too."

As Bennett walked out, Perry said, "See, she's still on that terrible treadmill we were on. She hasn't discovered the freedom that being poor can give you." Perry shook her head and said, "I so hope it happens for her someday."

◆

the unthinkable: You have failed to document each moment of your child's life. 'Fess up, sister: You're a slacker. You always were a slacker, muddling your way through college and the brief "job" you had, and motherhood didn't change a damn thing. But now you don't have to look like one, with **Scrappers for Slackers. Scrappers for Slackers** will hunt through every stray computer file, every tagged photo at your cousin's graduation party, every dusty side closet and desk drawer for some evidence of your child's life. Then with the magic of Photoshop, we'll construct a picture-perfect, expertly bound scrapbook that screams, "This child was in no way, shape, or form a big drunken mistake." Give us a call. You may be a slacker, but you're no Casey Anthony. Let **Scrappers for Slackers** prove it.

◆

Child Precocious in Sarcasm

Suburgatory, USA—A local child has both impressed and alarmed his teachers with his precocious fluency in sarcasm.

Tex Holter attends the Mason Elementary School. His teacher, Jared Bauer, is bowled over by his abilities and describes the first time he became aware of Tex's sarcastic talents.

"He's *six years old*. And yet he overheard me saying Principal Massey accidentally sent out an embarrassing personal e-mail to the whole staff and, without missing a beat, said—I shit you not—'Awkward!' and walked away."

At first, Bauer and others thought it was a fluke, but it was not.

"One day a specialist came in to help one of the disabled kids in the class. This specialist is just a bumbling idiot. Of course, what do the kids know? Well, one of them knows; Tex Holter knows. He sees her and says, 'Oh great, *that* one.'"

But Holter's strange fluency in sarcasm has a serious downside. It sets him well apart from his classmates, according to Bauer. "These are six-year-olds. Their idea of a joke is to put the word 'poop' at the end of every sentence and then say, 'Get it? Poop. Get it? Poop. Get it? Poop.' Again and again. That's normal—and annoying after a few minutes, by the way—but the kids love it and laugh and laugh. So what does a kid like Tex do with that? They keep yelling 'poop!' in his face waiting for him to laugh and he just says, 'Talk to the hand.' So yeah, he's become a total outsider and we're worried about him. And I shouldn't have said 'a kid like Tex.' I've never met another one like him. I've seen more albinos than I've seen this."

The school took action to help protect Tex, allowing him to join the teacher's lunchroom. Now he has become fully conversant in school gossip and has become such a welcome source of humor among the teachers that they would be sad to see him go. "We know, we know, he needs to negotiate how to get along with his peers, but when I told him once that he was my own personal Jay Leno, he just gave me this stare and said, 'I'm with Coco,' meaning I had insulted him by choosing Leno instead of Conan, who I guess he thinks is far superior. Oh God, I laughed so hard."

The school felt it was crucial to pull Holter's parents into the mix to try to understand what's going on with their son. So Ben and Teresa Holter came in for a talk with teacher Jared Bauer.

Jared: *So I just want to say that I love having Tex in my class and he's a great kid, but he seems to have this unusually, um, developed way with humor, a kind of sarcasm that is very atypical for his age.*

Teresa [rolling her eyes]: *Right, we wouldn't want him to excel in anything, just try to make him mediocre like the rest of them.*

Ben: *Zing!*

Jared: *Ummmm, OK . . . it's just that his strange, I mean, extraordinary ability is causing him social problems.*

Ben: *Oh, like Bill Gates had problems? Yeah, he turned out just awful.*

Jared: *Sorry? Not quite understanding either of you.*

Ben: *Are you new here?*

Jared: *Huh?*

Ben: *Great, you're going to force me to speak in your language with all its ugly directness. We as a family are fluent in sarcasm, it's our primary language, our culture, our mother tongue. Tex is just doing what he was born to do. So what do you suggest be done?*

Jared: *Wow. Weird, never heard of this one. Well, I think we need to stop accommodating for Tex's "different ability" and force him back with his peers, or he'll never learn to speak and interact well with kids his age.*

Teresa: *Yeah, it's always been my dream that Tex think up the wittiest poop joke; yours too, Ben?*

Ben: *Harvard weights quality of poop jokes right alongside SAT scores.*

Jared: *Listen you two, Harvard's a long long way off. Right now I just want to make sure Tex makes some friends and finds a supportive group to thrive in.*

And with that, Teresa began a "slow clap."

As the meeting ended, Jared Bauer said, "Wow, that was brutal. What's cute and funny on a six-year-old is pure D-Bag on a forty-year-old. I'm going to help Tex with every fiber of my being to knock some of that smarm out of his system. 'Culture,' my ass. Poor kid!"

Bauer has his work cut out for him. When he told Tex that he could no longer have lunch with the teachers in the faculty lounge, he added, "Tex, we just think it's best for you to be with kids your age, to try to fit in and be with the regular boys." Tex stood there, in his ironic NOBODY PUTS BABY IN A CORNER T-shirt, and said, "Epic FAIL."

◆

Mom "Never Yells" at Kids, Uses Scorn Instead

Suburgatory, USA—A local mom prides herself on never yelling, preferring to use pointed scorn instead.

"Those people who yell, they should be hauled off to protective services. Don't they know what they're doing to their kids? I never even raise my voice when my—" Gina Burke's four-year-old daughter interrupted. "Mama, can I have a cup of water? I'm, I'm thwirsty now."

Gina took a very big breath, as if winding up, clenched her jaw and slowly articulated each word. "Right, Anna. I would just *love*. To get up. And get you something. Right after I sat down. Right after I *asked* you. If you needed something. It would be *so so* much fun for me. To get up. Again."

She got up in a huff and continued speaking about the lasting legacy yelling can have on children. "I grew up in a yelling household and I flinch every time I hear a raised voice. I simply never do it, in any context, no matter my frustration level. In fact, I won't let my kids even go to a house where I know the parent yells. My kids would just shut down, crumble."

In fact, what Gina doesn't know is that she is a mom whispered about by other parents for her "terrifying" discipline style. "I just don't have any reference point for it—I find it astonishing! It's so carefully thought out, and designed for maximum damage, like she's tossing an emotional shit bomb in her kids' faces," said friend Madeleine Golden.

Said another mom, "In every other way she is Miz Model-Mommy, I mean, she acts like if they were to eat a single non-organic blueberry, they'd keel over and die. But then she talks to them like that? I'd rather send my kid for a playdate with the creepy single guy next door to her who looks like Dog the Bounty Hunter, that's how bad I think she is."

Back at the Burke's home, Kenneth had just asked his mother if she could buy him a new Lego Star Wars kit.

Gina breathed deep again, and clenched. She picked up Anakin and Obi Wan and quietly but intensely started to playact with them. "'What do you think, Anakin?' 'Well, Obi Wan, I think Kenneth is pretty selfish when he knows we don't have the money to buy another Lego set.' 'Yeah, Anakin, and does Kenneth ever pick up the ones he already has?' 'No, Obi Wan, he sure is a spoiled rotten Sith Lord.'"

Kenneth just stared at his mother as Gina got up to make lunch. While Anna fussed, Gina said, "This must be why I spent eight years getting a PhD, so that I could cut happy faces out of sandwiches. Dreams do come true!"

At this point, Anna is too young to understand what her mother is getting at, and Kenneth just thinks "Mama is mad." But Gina's oldest, fourteen-year-old Kendra, fully understands what's behind her mother's "technique." She stated her take on this: "My mother. Is mad. That we. Ruined. Her professional. Ambitions. We didn't. She did that. Herself. And she. Can bite. My. Ass."

◆

SHOUT OUT

Join Our Weirdo Junior League!

Jenny Jorgenson is a mom and self-described "freeganista" who lives on Blanco Street.

We, as "freeganistas," take to the Shout Out today not just to scorn your throw-away culture, with your constant visits to big box stores and relentless focus on regular bathing. We want to win you over, too.

(Just to clarify. We are not "frugalistas," a term that has been overused to the point of becoming a pathetic Great Recession cliché. Frugalistas, put simply, are pussies. Only when you scavenge for completely free items can you truly disconnect from America's nauseating consumer culture. We are *freeganistas*. Not trite at all, right?)

Though I do enjoy scorning this culture of waste, I wanted to show the human side of dumpster diving and scouring this great town for free items. My freeganista adventures have brought me far more than untold savings and one admittedly nasty case of intestinal worms. Freegan living has brought me firmly into the fold of what I call our town's Weirdo Junior League. Trust me, they're the only people worth knowing within a hundred miles.

The Weirdo Junior League is centered at the town dump, which is in essence a free garage sale. It's stuff that the corporate-controlled shopper-slaves drop off—perfectly good items—so they can resume their cycle of shop and dump and shop and dump in hopes of forgetting the futility of their lives and the inevitability of death. Meanwhile, my Weirdo Junior League members are eating their lunch, sometimes literally!

My Disabled Home-Boy

An emotionally disabled man who regularly visits the dump with his aide taught me that the band Journey is a great unifier; I was afraid he was going to wrestle that *Frontiers* cassette out of my hand (being a freeganista means, of course, that your decade-old car still has a cassette player).

The Vagitarian

Her bumper sticker says, I'M A VAGITARIAN. Even better would have been PUSSY. IT'S WHAT'S FOR DINNER. I saw her once at Dunkin' Donuts, so she is apparently a Donutarian, too, a proclivity to which I could relate. Did you know that Dunkin' Donuts server Mariela will give you all their leftovers at 6:00 p.m.? And the donuts freeze beautifully!

Now if only we could get the gay guy in town who has the bumper sticker, ROCK OUT WITH YOUR COCK OUT, and our little Weirdo Junior League would be homosexually complete. I should be honest, I have never had the balls to talk to the Vagitarian, because she looks a little mad all the time. Sometimes I'm a real bottom that way. Maybe she needs more veg. I mean, Vag!

Haunted House Guy

Every town's got at least one, right? This guy's "home" is packed floor to ceiling with, well, what in the Sam Hill is in there? Oh yeah, crap from the dump. All I know is it's busting out the windows, and no wonder both of his neighbors have their houses on the market. He's one of those crazy people who is sweet and exasperating in equal parts—also grimy, which I love, and buoyant. And he has a real touch with kids, finding magic everywhere in the unexpected. If he wasn't so clearly deranged, I'd have him babysit.

Beryl the Yenta

As a daily attendee at the dump, Beryl is like the Elder Stateswoman of town secrets. One man's trash is another man's treasure? Actually one man's trash is another lady's *gossip*. What do you think happens when an old wedding album tragically appears at the dump? Trust me, word spreads fast— like, Twitter-fast—and she doesn't own a single texting device! If you think you're hiding anything when you dump your crap, just ask Beryl. She could give you a profile of your life like what you might see on the show *Criminal Minds*. Seriously, it will make your hair stand on end. Shred before you dump. Beryl's on to you.

Freecyclers

This is a website where you post items you can offer to others to come pick up, bits and bobs you'd end up chucking in a landfill. Through freecycling, I've met a saintly foster mom and a few delightful junkster shut-ins. Here are some of my favorite offerings from freecyclers.

Offer: Ovaltine. We have promised this twice and it is still here. Please, for the LOVE come get the Ovaltine. It is starting to develop a complex. It's a really nice 12 oz. jar. I hope someone out there can give it a good home.

—Miserable (Ovaltine) in Marlborough

Offer: Gynecologist examining chair from maybe the 1940s. Your grandma might have been examined in this!

Offer: Extra progesterone vaginal suppositories for hormone replacement.

Do you have any idea how much those suppositories cost retail? I hope someone snagged them.

And sometimes being Super-Crazy-Mega-Cheap brings friends closer together.

One day recently, a friend, PTO goddess Laura Beazley, who is not in the Weirdo Junior League (not yet, anyway) looked over at me, and, knowing I had just gone on a thrifting adventure that week, started laughing uncontrollably. "What?" I asked. She pointed at my outfit and said, "That's my shirt! The shirt I left at the dump! You found my shirt!"

It's a freeganista miracle!

◆

Five-Year-Old Loves, But No Longer "In Love with," Mommy

Suburgatory, USA—A five-year-old boy "loves" but is no longer "in love" with his mommy, and thinks she has grown "needy and possessive."

Evan Morton was in a reflective mood about his situation while sitting in his Batman Underoos at the kitchen island, nursing the last of his Horizon Organic Chocolate Milk Box. "See?" he said, pointing at the label certifying the milk as antibiotic-, pesticide-, and hormone-free. "See, what good care she takes of me? God, this is hard. So, so hard."

He gestured in a defeated way to his dad, who was at the refrigerator. "Dad, can I get another one of these?"

"Comin' right up, Ev," his dad replied.

According to Morton, he and Mommy have been together for five years. "Let's be honest. Early on I was in it just for the boobs. That first year, it was all boobs, all the time, all I wanted and needed. I didn't really look at her as a person. I know I sound awful for saying that, but it's true. She was more like some . . . thing . . . attached to those wonderful boobs." He sucked down the last of the second chocolate milk.

"Listen, Dad." He belched. "Good one, right?"

His dad said, "Good one, buddy!"

Morton went on. "But eventually she was more than boobs. In years two, three, and four, the relationship deepened. She gave me solid food, and we really connected as human beings. We were really communicating. Seeing her face lit me up like nothing else. I'll never forget our first visit to Bugaboo Creek together—my choice, of course—to see the robot moose. We laughed together so hard. Sounds silly now. Sad too," he said.

"You OK, Ev?" his dad asked.

"Yeah, I'm alright. Anyway, yes, I was in love with her. Me and her and no one else. Well, at that point there was also Bob the Builder and Thomas the Tank Engine and Diego, and, I'm embarrassed to admit, The Wiggles, but at that time if I had to make the choice between Bob and Tom and Diego and The Wiggles and her, I would have chosen her."

Morton moved out to the living room and flipped on the TV. *Power Rangers: Samurai* was on. "Yes!" He did the same frenetic dance he always does when the opening sequence of *Power Rangers* comes on, which involves cartwheels, handstands, fist thrusts, and running around in a circle.

As he sacked out to watch *Power Rangers*, Morton started to describe how things have been going downhill for the two of them. "She's *so* needy and possessive. You know, after school I want to play the Pip Penguin Club with my boys. We're space penguins who kill zombies who are trying eat our space brains. It's *really* important to me. It's my thing, it's what I do. She demeans it. And she is always embarrassing me in front of my buds and dragging me home. Then she's pissed and doesn't get it when she asks, 'Why don't your friends like meeeeee?'"

Also, Morton believes her nagging is taking a real toll. "She's always asking me, 'Are you going to wear that Clone Wars T-shirt *again?*' 'Yes I am, Mommy, until freedom is restored to the galaxy, and General Grievous and Count Dooku are taken down, YES I AM. *What* does it matter to you?' Or with the food, always the food. 'Eat your gummy Vites. Just try these eggie-eggs, just once.' I mean, do I *look* like the kind of guy who wants to eat tofu? I ask her, 'How does this even affect you?' Then she starts crying and telling me it's because she loves me more than life itself, and it's just awful, and, hey, I'm not made of stone."

At that point, Morton heard his Mommy come in with groceries. She walked in and said, "Hey, handsome!" Morton looked at her and said, "hey." She came over to give him at least ten kisses and to ruffle his hair, while Morton squirmed away. "God, that was awkward, wasn't it? Sorry you had to see that." Morton said, cringing.

"What do you want to do tonight?" she asked.

"*Cats and Dogs: The Revenge of Kitty Galore* is on," Morton replied.

"OK, well, we are going to Bertucci's, so maybe it will be on when we get back. You've been in those Underoos all day. Go change!" Mommy said.

Morton groaned and stomped upstairs. "Yeah, I'm annoyed. But I still know, when all is said and done, that she's a wonderful woman. Who I still love. Who probably deserves better," he said, pulling out his Clone Wars T-shirt from the hamper. "NOT the Clone Wars T-Shirt *again*, Evan!" she yelled from downstairs.

◆

Dad: Guppies Represent "Everything that's Wrong with America"

Suburgatory, USA—A dad is telling his daughter that the guppies in their home represent "everything that's wrong with America."

Greg Mazur, forty-nine, recently lost his job as sales manager at the Piermont Insurance Company and now is spending more time at home with his ten-year-old daughter, Ava.

"Time to feed the freeloaders!" Mazur said, grabbing the fish food to shake into the aquarium.

"God, it's like Sodom and Gomorrah in there. Ughhh . . . disgusting," said Mazur. Ava has been noticing that her dad now gets agitated every time he has to feed the guppies, a community of dozens that grew from a single guppy brought home from school last year. "Yeah, that first guppy slut must have been knocked up when Ava brought her home," said Mazur quietly.

Ava: *Daddy, why are you so mad at the guppies?*

Mazur: *Well, sweetie, because I look in there and see everything that is wrong with America. You know, when Mommy and Daddy decided to have you and your brother, we planned it out and made sure we could swing it, money-wise. But look at these guppies, do you think they plan anything? They just have guppy after guppy after goddamn guppy, I mean do they think they have any chance of paying for, I don't know, college?*

Ava: *Daddy, guppies don't have college.*

Mazur: *But if they* did, *all these little babies, they'd be out of luck wouldn't they?*

Ava: *What does it matter?*

Mazur: *What does it matter? What matters is that they are relying on us to feed them, money out of our pockets, stuck paying for their bad life choices.* [muttering] *Welfare queens. . . .*

Ava: *What's a welfare queen?*

Mazur [muttering]: *They're guppies who can't keep their legs together. See there's no respect for life in there. They swim around in their own poop and pee. Diseases all over the place—white spot disease, gold dust disease, fish lice, dropsy. Those are* lifestyle *diseases, Ava. You* choose *to get them because you don't take care of yourself.*

Ava: *Daddy, if it's dirty in there, that's* our *fault.*

Mazur: *Right, it's always our fault. I repeat—no respect for life. These people eat their own. Once they shoot them out they don't even bother with taking care of them.*

Ava: *But Daddy, that's what Miss Dalton said they're* supposed *to do; this is nature.*

Mazur: *That's fine for Miss Dalton, but we don't have to like it, or celebrate it.* [muttering] *Typical liberal bullshit they feed my kids. That's why they hand out these guppies. Start trainin' 'em early to hand over their hard-earned cash to a bunch of lazy thugs.*

Ava [defiantly]: *I love my guppy family.*

Mazur [muttering]: *Family. Like the Manson Family maybe or some filthy commune. Seriously, Ava, does that look like any family you've ever seen? How many are in there? Do they know who their fathers are? Who are the moms?*

Ava: *The moms are the fat ones.*

Mazur [triumphantly]: *Bingo.*

At that point, Mazur's wife Emily came home, walked in, and kissed Ava and said, "Oh no, has Daddy been yelling at the guppies again? Greg, ease up on the poor guppies! They didn't lay you off from your job, you know. Did you put in for unemployment today? Or just yell at the guppies again?"

"Ummmm," Mazur said, looking dejected.

"Greg. Honey," she said, hands in the air.

"OK, right. I'll do it. We'll be OK," he said, shaking more fish food into the aquarium.

◆

Dr. Drama

"When life hands you a problem, let's make it more interesting!"

Dear Dr. Drama:

I'm afraid my husband might be gay. He doesn't seem to have much interest in me, you know, **that way,** and he just seems a lot more, um, fixated on the dads when we go to school events or soccer games. Also, and I know I shouldn't have done this, but I looked at his search history on the computer and found gay porn! And then I found a strange number on his cell phone that came up a lot, I called it, and it was a man. Do you think he might be gay? He's my best friend, I don't want to lose him!

—Paranoid in Suburgatory

Dear Paranoid:

Your subconscious is screaming at you, and your conscious is covering its ears and yelling "La la la. I can't see the big fag sleeping right next to me!", so I'll say it loud and clear for you: Your husband is gay. You can pretend all you want that just being a *little curious about gay porn doesn't mean anything, but take it from another sucker like me: Where there's gay porn and a mystery man, there's a late night circle jerk or early morning gym tug fest not far behind. Then he'll settle down, find that special guy, and have a beautiful gay wedding you won't be invited to.*

Now if this was Oprah hell-bent on offering a happy ending in that final ten minutes of the show, she'd be telling you to "get some therapy, figure out what's really going on, maybe sex isn't the most important thing in the world if this is your best friend." But Dr. Drama is Old Testament all the way. Retribution, not redemption, that's my bible. He stole your most potent sexual years! So here's what you do. Tell your "best friend" that he can still be your best gay friend, but pack his bags right now and tell him to get the hell out. Don't worry about the kids, it might be hard at first, but gay dads make the greatest dads, once they're getting it up the ass, which is what they've been dreaming about the whole time. So eventually, they'll be fine. And while he's packing, you're going to put on your best tramp outfit, and you're going out, driving into the big city, getting hammered, and getting fucked by someone who loves vagina. Your vagina, and all vaginas. This is your moment. It was stolen from you. Steal it back.

◆

"America the So-So" Campaign Mars Fourth of July Celebration

Suburgatory, USA—A group promoting the slogan "America the So-So" caused a ruckus at the annual Fourth of July celebration on the town green, which attracts a more diverse crowd from several different towns.

Dave Sheehan runs the bipartisan advocacy group, American Realists for a Real America. "We get accused a lot of being unpatriotic, which just . . . ugh . . . makes me crazy. And I'm a Republican! So we thought putting 'America' in twice might help."

Sheehan's group is committed to puncturing some of the illusions Americans might have about just how "great" America really is, and he feels he was too mild for the Tea Party's hard-edge. "I won't yell at people or name-call, but I am determined to tell it like it is. A true patriot looks himself in the eye and says, 'You can't change what you don't acknowledge!'"

Sheehan is referring to Life Law Number 4 as expounded by the inspiration behind American Realists for a Real America—Dr. Phil. Sheehan, who's been out of full-time work for eight months, took Dr. Phil's "get real" message to heart, and began to see that the true enemy of America was self-delusion. That's why Sheehan chose the Fourth of July to roll out the group's slogan: "America the So-So."

"I wanted something a lot stronger, but I figured I'd pull more people in, then boom! Rock 'em, sock 'em with my pamphlets," he said.

Sheehan explains the trouble with America. "Math skills, life expectancy, roads and bridges, our debt rating, bungled wars, obesity, you name it, when you consider how rich we are, we're in a death spiral. America the Great? It's just not true. And yet the thing we come in Number 1 on over and over again? Self-regard."

Was there anything he could think of that America does well?

Sheehan watched a man bite into a giant sausage-and-peppers hoagie, while his son pressed a sugar-coated fried dough to his face.

"Eat well? And look how great that's going!"

Sheehan had set up his booth with his "America the So-So" sign, handing out pamphlets he had prepared, a veritable library of doom. He had "Nation of the Living Dead—America's Demographic Timebomb," "Rotting Stump: The Sugaring of America's Life-Blood," and "War and the Military Meat-Grinder," among others.

The same man who had just finished his hoagie looked at the sign and the pamphlets, and said, "What the fuck is this shit? You know it's the Fourth of July, right? Are you a fucking Communist? You know, I am a veteran of the Iraq war *and* I have diabetes."

Sheehan said, "Sir, 'America the So-So' is my own patriotic way of saying America needs to . . ." He looked at the man's stomach. ". . . shape up. That's 'getting real.' That's loving America."

The man was fuming. "Asswipe. It's America the *Beautiful*. Put your hand over your heart or go the fuck home. Or better yet, get a one way ticket to . . . Kenya."

The fireworks began. Sheehan looked up at the patriotic display and said, "The cost of every one of these colorful little explosions could have fed a hungry orphan in Kenya for months. But, well, I still love you, America, you batty old broad! Happy Birthday!"

As he packed up his booth, he said, "Well, I guess that only went so-so, right?" He laughed ruefully at his own attempt at a joke. "Still if I can open only one person's mind, it's worth it." But was he offering any solutions to these problems, beyond getting real?

"Actually I haven't had a chance to get beyond Dr. Phil's Life Law Number 4, but we'll have more time now that our big debut is over."

In the spirit of puncturing self-delusions, this reporter was a bit suspicious and curious as to who the "we" was in American Realists for a Real America, since Sheehan was very much alone all day. It turns out that his only outlet, on Facebook, has just three Facebook fans: Sheehan, his wife, and one man with no picture named Gene Juluca. When presented with this news, Sheehan, rather than being embarrassed, said, "You just might have what it takes to be an American Realist for a Real America!"

And who is Gene Juluca? "Oh, that's the Facebook page for my kid's stuffed monkey."

◆

The Following Is a Paid Political Announcement

Vote Billie Carson for Mayor

As a longstanding exercise bulimic, I know your community better than most. Whether it's the dangerous rocks that need rearranging on the Brook Path or dismantling that deadly Rotary on Atwood Road, I don't need to get up to speed on the issues facing our town. Oh, I'm up to speed—on high speed, a speed like you wouldn't believe possible by a menopausal woman.

I am also one of the best-known, and surely one of the best-loved faces in this great little patch of America. In fact, one time, I even heard a boy shout out of his car, "Look, Mommy, there's the flying skeleton with the big head!" Well, son, that comment meant the world to this flying skeleton. My name is Billie Carson, and I'm asking for your mom and dad's vote for Mayor

November 3rd. Come to the police station this Saturday, where we'll have a wonderful lunch of bread-free lettuce and mustard sandwiches and pickles. I'll even take a break to stationary jog, all to hear my constituents' most pressing concerns!

So Vote Billie Carson. I simply won't stop pounding the pavement on your behalf.

◆

Dad and Hot Nanny
Really Just Good Friends

Suburgatory, USA—A local dad and a hot nanny are "really just good friends."

"Hi, Mr. H!" said vivacious and buxom Mandy Mistrall, eighteen, a nanny wearing daisy dukes and high-heeled sneakers and licking a large lollipop.

"Mandy! I know you're planning to wash the car, but it's so hot out; why don't we get you out of that shirt?" said Rock Hardt, a father of two who hired Mistrall days after she turned eighteen.

"Mandy's had a bit of a rocky road in her path to becoming a nanny. Her father walked out on her and now she has what I think they call 'daddy issues.' Good thing I found her. Now she has someone strong and nurturing attending to all her needs."

Was she experienced? "No, she was a completely fresh, unspoiled virgin to the job at hand. We decided to overlook some trouble she had fallen into at the Reform School for Wayward Girls. Let's just say our Mandy is innocent, but a bit of a vixen. We know now after much more experience with the issue that Mandy was just getting in touch with her emerging bisexuality. The tickle fights in the girls' shower area at the school got a little out of control. That's how she ended up on the side of the road that fateful night."

Mistrall, sudsing up the car with long methodical strokes while sprawled out on the hood of the car, describes meeting Mr. H. "It's a really funny story. It was a stormy night and I was stranded on the side of the road. I was soaking wet. Good thing Mr. H had an extra shirt with him. It was really big and that worked out well, of course, because he didn't have extra pants. We were stuck in the car for many hours and really had some special intimate time getting to know each other better."

Now Mistrall is part of the family and, as Rock Hardt put it, "up for anything," which is really important in the freewheeling Hardt household.

"With my wife now confined to a wheelchair, Mandy is so nice to oil up my sore muscles when I need it, which is to say, often," said Hardt.

Mistrall finished the car and came in to change. She emerged an hour later in thigh-high boots and a micro-mini. "Don't you look just good enough to eat, Mandy!" said Hardt.

Two other similarly attired and similarly vivacious and buxom girls arrived. "Enjoy your three-way!" Hardt said.

Three-way? "Three-way date. What did you think I meant?"

This reporter wondered if having such an attractive nanny, along with an infirm wife, presented Hardt with perhaps too much temptation.

Rock Hardt was aghast. "First of all this is a *barely legal* girl you are talking about. And second, that is such a silly cliché from, well, I think you must be watching por-nography! It appears that *someone* here, not me, has a very dirty mind. What kind of journalism school did you go to, anyway?"

◆

Heartwarming Herpes Tale Brings a Family Together

Suburgatory, USA—In a heartwarming tale of first-lust, untreatable sores, and eventual redemption, a four-year-old has discovered how the two people he calls "Mommy" and "Daddy" became a family. And in the telling, they all learned what really matters in life.

It began when Devon Corrie spotted the so-called "tramp stamp" tattoo on "Mommy"—Eve Corrie—which became visible when Corrie was fumbling with the attach-ments on the vacuum.

As she bent over, Devon saw a strange picture on Cor-rie's lower back. "Mommy, what is that? There's a picture of a naked lady on your back! She's in a garden and there's, there's, there's . . . a snake! Mommy, it has the letters E-V-E." It was a tattoo of a sexed-up Eve with metalhead hair in the Garden of Eden.

"Yeah, Mommy's pretty hot, isn't she?" said Rich Corrie.

"Rich, stop! You want him running around saying "Mommy's hot, Mommy's hot?"

"So Mommy, what does E-V-E spell?" asked Devon. Eve Corrie gave her son that look that says, "Isn't my child the most adorable moron?"

Corrie said, "Eve's my name, sweetie! You have a name, Devon. And Mommy's name is Eve."

Devon looked at her, utterly confused. "But you are Mommy. Mommy Corrie."

"Well of course I'm Mommy, but before you were born, Mommy wasn't a mommy yet. Back then I was just Eve. I had a life before you were born."

"Oh did she ever!" Rich Corrie couldn't resist interrupting.

"Rich. Your son is confused and I'm trying to explain. Mommy existed. Mommy was a person. Mommy had, well, I had a lot of, what should we call it, um, bad fun before you came into my life and made me Mommy. But you can forget about Eve, that's not me anymore. I'll never set foot on that boardwalk again," said Eve, actually starting to tear up.

"Why are you crying, Mommy? Don't cry!" Devon ran up to her and started to console her.

"Eve, it's OK, honey! Let me give it a try," Rich said, turning to Devon. "Mommy is sad because when Mommy was Eve she, um, had some bad fun when she went out for a playdate one night on the boardwalk. She made a friend who liked bad fun, too, and who left Mommy with a nasty bug she can never, ever get rid of."

Eve Corrie, muttering, said, "Oh my God you just told our child that his mom is a dirty herpes whore."

"But you know what Daddy thinks?" said Rich Corrie. "Daddy thought Eve was the most fun, most funny, most beautiful, and most wonderful girl he'd ever met. And Mommy is exactly the same, except now we have you, and it's more wonderful than ever, except for the times now and then when the itchy painful sores come out." Eve began tearing up again.

Devon still looked confused, and said, "How did Mommy get those nasty itchy sores?"

Rich and Eve looked at each other. "Well this is probably not going to make much sense but the friend she met who loved the bad fun? Well, that was your Daddy. I was 'Rich' back then and I had just met Mommy that night on the boardwalk and I gave the nasty bug to her. I have it, too."

"You two didn't wash your hands, did you!" Devon said, thrilled to have caught his parents having bad fun.

"You're right, we didn't protect ourselves from that nasty bug. But at the same time Daddy gave me the nasty bug, he also gave me *you*. He became Daddy that night of bad fun," Eve said.

"So if that was a mistake, Devon, thank God, because it was the best mistake I ever made. What really matters in life is love. And family," she said.

"And Valtrex," Rich said. "Herpes may be forever, but family is, too," as they gathered in a warm three-way embrace.

◆

Boy Loves Steve Jobs More than Parents

Suburgatory, USA—A twelve-year-old boy loves Steve Jobs "way more" than his parents, a development that's been years in the making and showing no signs of ebbing away.

"That smug, know-it-all motherfucker!" said Phil Macon of Apple founder Steve Jobs. "That guy has singlehandedly ruined my relationship with my son!"

Just as Phil finished his rant, "Steve Jobs," as his son Benno will now only answer to, walked into the room, holding his Steve Jobs plush toy.

"Hello, Father," he said coolly, with a somewhat dreamy countenance.

"Hello, Steve," Phil said, choking out the name with hate in his voice.

Macon dates his son's fandom back at least six years, when he realized that his son was calling himself "Steve Jobs," choosing to wear a black turtleneck and jeans and even sleeping in the outfit.

"All I did was want a stupid iPod. And yes, I took Benno to the Apple Store with me. It was like he walked in and thought 'This is my real and true family.' Like a very very clean religious cult where there are no moms and no dads, just a gang of self-satisfied little fucks. That Apple Store is now like, like his sacred temple and his God is a charisma-bot—named Steve Jobs."

Phil Macon said that the cost of acquiring the latest Apple gear is bankrupting the family, but it's what has happened to Benno's personality that's the hardest pill to swallow. "He's become . . . I can't believe I'm saying this about my own kid, but he's become a dick. He'd throw his own parents overboard in a heartbeat if it meant saving Steve Jobs from whatever disease it is he has."

Phil Macon says his own appearance doesn't help matters either. "Yeah, look at me. Think about it. Who do I look like? A little schlubby, dirty-blond hair, wearing my 'lame' glasses and 'lame' pleated khakis? Yep—dead ringer for the PC Guy from those unbelievably obnoxious Mac-PC Guy ads. Benno even printed out a *picture* for me that said, 'How to Dress Like a PC Guy,' the dude was all decked out in clothes from Sears. Benno handed it to me, without a word, like he was quietly slipping me a giant shit sandwich. It's not even that he thinks I'm the enemy, his 'PC guy' dad. He thinks I'm *pathetic*."

This reporter spoke with "Little Steve Jobs," who was a bit worn out after watching the World Wide Developers' Conference the night before—the must-see event for Jobs' fanatics where they not only worship the new products and features discussed, but also obsessively scrutinize Jobs's appearance for signs of health and vitality.

As is his custom, the day after WWDC, Benno was ritually rewatching previous WWDC presentations. What does he love so much about Steve Jobs? He laughed smoothly. "You mean what do I love about myself? That's immodest . . . don't you think? Really my role in the world is quite simple, spare, and elegant. I want to put a 'ding in the universe' and I think I'm achieving that. Don't you?" he said, gesturing to the array of devices on his desk.

Does it bother him that his parents feel shoved aside by his Steve Jobs fandom? "I really do care for those people, but I simply won't engage in petty jealousies when so many exciting discoveries are yet to be made. Really, if you look at, say, Father, he should perhaps start thinking about his own health and appearance. As you can see, he is looking a bit . . . dated."

When told of Benno's statement, Phil Macon exploded. "You see?"

"Little Steve Jobs" admitted that there have been long-time strains with his "parents," using air quotes while saying "parents."

"Of course, I do appreciate them taking me in when I needed a family, but I suspect my birth parents might have been a bit more . . . visionary. More Silicon Valley campus than suburban office park."

Confused, this reporter consulted with the real Steve Jobs's Wikipedia page and saw that he was born in 1955 and given up for adoption.

◆

Go the F*ck to Sleep?
Meet Get a F*cking Life

Suburgatory, USA—Annoyed by the barely sublimated parental rage found in the smash bestseller, *Go the F*ck to Sleep* by Adam Mansbach, a child sensation has penned an acidic rejoinder called, *Get a F*cking Life.*

"We as kids just thought we needed our own potty-mouth satirical send-up that expresses *our* frustrations—and believe me, we have many," said nine-year-old phenom author Patrick Bryson. "As *Go the F*ck to Sleep* so ably demonstrates, the child-parent relationship is fraught with complexities. We hope *Get a F*cking Life* honors those complexities while also giving everyone a five- or even seven-minute chuckle."

Bryson is considered an up-and-comer, named by the *New Yorker* as one of its "10 under 10" young writers to watch. "We expect *Get a F*cking Life* to be *the* gift for Father's Day, Mother's Day, any time you want to give Mom and Dad a little zing," said Bryson.

This reporter was fortunate enough to get a sneak preview of *Get a F*cking Life*, which is already zooming up the bestseller list months before publication. And Bryson allowed us to excerpt it here.

When your day is bleak . . . and you need some peace . . . and you find it in a box of wine . . . I come to you, Mommy, lift you from the floor, and say: Get a F*cking Life.

When I sit in your lap . . . at the day's end . . . see the porno on the iPad screen . . . I cup your face, Daddy, with my little hands and say: Get a F*cking Life.

Our weekends unspool . . . like a cat pulling yarn . . . you telling Dad, "You ruined my life." And Dad saying, "You ruined mine, too, you f*cking shrew!" I curl at your feet and say: Get a F*cking Life.

Come Sunday night . . . I don't have the blues . . . I count the minutes till I can return to school . . . where I feel safe with Miss Kenney . . . far away from you. And I say, one last time, to Mommy and Dad: Get a F*cking Life.

Where did Bryson come up with his material? "As with any writer, I have mined my personal experience. Oh, and the family court documents after my parents' divorce, too. That thing was huge! Turns out, I had blocked out a lot. Authenticity is key."

Just as *Go the F*ck to Sleep* enlisted a celebrity, Samuel L. Jackson to voice some of the story, Bryson brought on Gilbert Gottfried, former voice of Aflac, who was let go from the insurance company after making inappropriate jokes after the Japanese earthquake. "We kids love him because he's the voice of Digit on *Cyberchase*. And his voice will drive my parents, I mean, all parents, out of their f*cking minds. Get it? I said 'fucking'! Adding "fuck" to anything is hilarious!"

◆

BRIARCLIFF ACADEMY—
Educating the Stupid Rich Since 1903
A message from Briarcliff Academy
Headmaster Mason Siegel

For the high net-worth individual who has attended the very best schools, there can be nothing more challenging than discovering that your child is stupid. That's why, for more than a century, **Briarcliff Academy** has catered exclusively to the needs of this overlooked and underserved population. At Briarcliff, our mission is clear: We endeavor to insulate your child from his or her own inadequacies, and insulate *you* from the harsh realities those inadequacies create.

In a world that is growing more complex by the minute, your child simply won't be able to keep up. We will arm you and your child with the skills needed to hide his or her stupidity with elegance and aplomb. Briarcliff's commitment to no academic standards and no testing means neither you nor your child will face the tyranny of the bad report card. Our emphasis on non-traditional learning and out-of-the-box thinking ensures that your child can accomplish something that requires little actual ability, but has all the hallmarks of real creative achievement.

How do we maintain the exclusivity that someone of your stature has come to expect? Besides our lush grounds and state-of-the-art facilities, the answer can be found on your first bill. With tuition priced twice as high as conventional private schools, you can be sure that your child will be among only the most elite of his stupid brethren. Scholarship children are not accepted because we cannot serve the needs of smart, poor children. But of course we welcome all races and religions as long as your child is stupid and rich. And as your child gets close to that exciting time to apply to college, our expert placement team will guide your child to the stupid rich college of her choice, where she will find a similarly select group of dim-witted, wealthy peers, without those taxing standards.

"The rich are different." The stupid rich don't know where that phrase comes from. And that's just fine with us. **Briarcliff Academy.**

◆

Playground Vagina, Loved and Loathed Town Landmark

Suburgatory, USA—The fight over the so-called Playground Vagina has come to a head as both sides war over the fate of a landmark either loved or loathed among squabbling townspeople.

It's unclear when exactly Playground Vagina came to be. "I mean there was this enclosed slide that the dads always thought looked like, you know, a vagina. We would joke about it," said Brad Silver.

"Yeah, we would look at all the kids rolling around in it and say, 'Hey that vag is seeing more action than Lindsay Lohan's! Or Paris Hilton's! Or Kim Kardashian's! Or whoever the fun slut of the moment is, you know?" said Harry Manwald.

"Then one day," said Silver, "it was like the smut gods smiled on us bored-out-of-our mind dads or something, and we arrived at the playground to see that someone, probably some teenage squirt, had written VAGINA right at the mouth of the slide. We laughed our asses off. That was a great day, wasn't it?" Manwald agreed. "Totally."

Carey Manheim didn't see it that way. She immediately assembled a group of moms to scrub the Vagina off. "We, as concerned moms, did not think that when we take our children to the playground anyone should be thinking about their genitals. That is the only purpose of Playground Vagina—to stimulate talk about the genitals and stimulate the genitals themselves."

The dads grumbled, and each side, the dads and the concerned moms, thought that was the end of that. But they were very wrong.

Angered by the removal of the first VAGINA, the playground prankster stepped it up a notch. The next phrase to appear was PINK TACO. "Oh God, we were high-fiving when we saw it, we loved it so much. And we could never have dreamed it would get even funnier," said Silver. And yes, over a series of six months, the following names appeared on the top of Playground Vagina, unleashing a cycle of removals and reappearances:

FURBURGER. Then JUICY BOX. Then MRS. FLUFFY. Then SPASM CHASM. And then, finally, the one that was both the dads' favorite and the final straw for the concerned moms, COOZ MCSLIMY.

At that point, the majority of moms thought the only solution was to remove the actual piece of equipment.

Manheim, the first mom to rail against Playground Vagina was surprisingly against the idea, arguing that the children shouldn't have to suffer from the actions of some filthy teenage boy.

The mystery was solved one night after a park supervisor realized he'd left his toolbox and returned to find Manheim, with spray can in hand. After she was fined by the police, Manheim was asked to explain her bizarre actions. "I'm bored out of my mind. These dads think they're bored out of their minds? They're only here a few times a week, not a few times a day." But why did she advocate removing the original VAGINA? "Oh, you know when you get away with something you get hungry for more? Like Anthony Weiner? That's me," said Manheim.

The dads, when they first saw Manheim again, were so in awe of her they could barely speak. The bravest among them said, "We didn't think girls . . . knew all those names." "You're forgetting I actually have a vagina!" And with that Manheim joined the brotherhood, having already been cast out by her old sister-moms.

◆

Little Loman's Lemonade Stand

Suburgatory, USA—A pint-sized Willy Loman is selling lemonade, Nilla wafers, and despair over on the corner of Cartwright Street and Elm.

"We're out there, baking in the sun, dreaming of closing a few measly sales, and what do we get? Dust in our face from the Caddies just whizzing by without a care in the world," declared sad-sack eight-year-old Jonah Miller.

"What's a caddie?" asked seven-year-old Abby Green, who'd do anything, anything in the world to save Miller from the terminal gloom that's descended on him these past two days of selling no more than two lemonades and one Nilla wafer. But mostly she has no idea what he's talking about.

"It's what the great man drives, doll, not you and not me," said Jonah.

Miller has spent much of the weekend manning the stand. And what a weekend it has been. It began with the exhilarating promise of little-boy riches and is ending with the dying dreams on the hard streets of a suburban town on the edge of a haunted future.

"I look around . . . I see these other lemonade stands . . . every one of them grabbing for just one tiny crumb off the delicious cake that is America. But what are we really in this for, this rat-race that takes a boy who gives his blood, sweat, and guts and eats him alive? Why Abby? Why?" Jonah implored.

"Because we wanted money to get tokens at Chuck E. Cheese, remember?" responded Abby.

"It isn't right, what kind of life is this, in the greatest town in the loudest country in the world?" Jonah questioned, putting his arms and head down on the stand.

Abby ran to get her mother. "You know, I could kick myself for even letting Abby and her weird friend Jonah set up that little dread-factory. I should have known that they'd be out there, just asking to get their hearts broken," said Peggy Green. "Everyone drives in suburbia. You know, his cousins Ben, Josh, and Daniel in New York set up a stand at 82nd and Madison—"Lempops"—and made, I'm not kidding, two hundred bucks in two hours? It wasn't even real lemonade! But here, the only people on the roads or side-walks are these psychotic runner-mommies, who wouldn't ever *think* of stopping to give these kids one moment of dignity. 'What, you want us to eat your fake lemonade and cardboard carb-laden poison cookies?' Well if it was your kid, you'd stop. I'm sure if it was a Botox stand they'd be lined up half a block long."

Green immediately put out the message—"Attention Must Be Paid" to locals on Facebook and Twitter, telling them if they didn't go out and buy a Dixie cup and a Nilla wafer *now*, they risked her unfriending and unfollowing. "And public backstabbing, too," she said.

When people finally started arriving, Jonah picked up his head slowly and seemed at least relieved, but by no means redeemed. Would he now ever consider a career in sales? Jonah took a deep, defeated breath. "No. There's only one place where a beaten soul can hold his head high and shoot for honor and esteem in a boy-eat-boy world, and that's behind the toy counter at Chuck E. Cheese."

◆

PAID ADVERTISER CONTENT

McCaskill Garden Design Presents . . . The Lawnzilian

Do you want your lawn to look like an old French whore? No? Then consider the very latest in cutting-edge landscape design: At McCaskill Garden Design, we're proud to present: **The Lawnzilian.**

Our patented **Lawnzilian** technique gives your lawn the closest, cleanest, and freshest cut you've ever seen.

Your grass is the first thing a stranger sees when entering your inner sanctum, your most special, private place. What will that first impression be? Will your guests and neighbors think, "This is someone who lets herself go. Who doesn't care about having an unkempt, unruly mess?" Or will they think, "*This* is someone who *takes care of business.*"

With **The Lawnzilian,** no thickets will tangle up your smooth, dewy sheen. No tufts will poke up from your concrete cracks. You can run, stray grass blades, but you can't hide from **The Lawnzilian!** A little nature is God's work. But too much nature is just plain disgusting. Act now, and receive a special offer, **The Fluffer-nator,** the soon-to-be patented technique to freshen up and re-energize even the most bone-dry of lawns. Call McCaskill Garden Design now!

◆

Anti-Vaxxer Barbie Doll Unveiled

Suburgatory, USA—Anti-vaccination activists have unveiled their latest ammunition in the battle to raise awareness of the harm they say that vaccines can cause: Anti-Vaxxer Barbie. The blond, amply proportioned anti-vaccination crusader spouts a number of slogans written by Charlotte Burger, head of the advocacy group Vaxxer Zappers, including:

Measles schmeasles.
Vax are whack.
Protect me, don't inject me.

Your gut knows, your pediatrician doesn't.
Think for yourself. Just say no.
Before you poke, Google it.
Pox or vax? I choose pox..

Burger demonstrated the doll, a retrofitted 1992 Teen Talk Barbie, with matted hair and a disheveled outfit. "I know she looks like, well, she's looking a little used, and the clothes are so dated. But we hope people focus on the important message that Anti Vaxxer Barbie is delivering." She began playing the doll, pushing the button on the back.

Vaccines—pushing poison.
Will I ever have enough clothes?

"Oh no," said Burger. "That last one isn't supposed to be in there. I thought we had gotten all the old Teen Talk Barbie phrases cleared out. Let's try again," she said.

No to the needle! No to the needle!
Wanna have a pizza party?

"Goddamn it!" Burger exploded, fumbling with the doll. "One more time."

Meet me at the mall!
Scientists don't know everything.
Big pharma, big bullies.
Math is hard!

The alternating phrases were made even more jarring because the original perky Barbie voice clashed dramatically with the harshly strident voice of Vaxxer Zapper Charlotte Burger.

"Ugh. We have a dad who tinkers with this kind of stuff, taking out the old computer chip and futzing around with it. We're really into 'do-it-yourself,' 'think-for-yourself,' but maybe we should have asked a professional or something," said Burger. She tried it one last time.

You vaccinate? Go fuck yourself, sheeple.

This reporter waited for an explanation, but Burger simply said, "Oh that one is supposed to be in there!"

When vaccine proponents got wind of Anti-Vaxxer Barbie, they commissioned a toy maker found on the homemade crafters' website Etsy to begin work on their own doll, a girl confined to a wheelchair in a world where childhood diseases are once again running rampant. They plan to call her "Polio Polly." Their doll will say, *"I wish my legs worked!"* and *"Why did hippies let polio come back?"*

When told of this development, Burger just threw up her hands and said, "You see? So overdramatic."

◆

Keller Piano Academy for the Low to Moderately Talented

Is your child showing a slight interest in music, but not necessarily the talent to take him to the heights of a career in piano? Then we might be just the school for you! At the **Keller Piano**

Academy for the Low to Moderately Talented, we will teach
your child to shoot, but only shoot just far enough. Gone is the
tension created when your piano teacher believes her student
will someday exceed her in ability or stature. It happens all the
time, and it's not pretty.

As the parent of a child with low to moderate talents in the
musical realm, you probably don't even *want* to get your kid lessons but are feeling the pressure. What would those bitches at
school say if you don't? You're not going to be one of *those
moms* who doesn't give your child every chance in life to excel,
are you?

Well, at the **Keller Piano Academy for the Low to Moderately Talented,** we will "teach" your child at cut-rate prices, and
you never have to worry about us secretly hating your beloved.

Because we'll let you in on a dirty little secret about piano
teachers: Most of us sit there during your child's lesson, dreaming of performing and wishing we didn't have that fucking mortgage to pay and maybe if we didn't have these bills and these
kids and that useless husband, we'd be prepping for Carnegie
Hall right now. When a superstar lands in our midst, burning
up the keyboard, all our hopes and dreams tickle past us like a
tragic arpeggio across our lives.

We get angry but can't show it, of course, because that
would be crazy, and so we engage in passive-aggressive sabotage. So if you have the next Lang Lang at home, the **Keller
Music Academy for the Low to Moderately Talented** is
probably not for you. But if you have the thoroughly average
child, our teachers might be the perfect fit to take him far in
his musical odyssey—but, well, not too far! We love seeing his
little fingers stumbling helplessly across the keyboard, never to
amount to much of anything beyond a robotic rendition of "Fur

Elise," which is probably all you want anyway. Call or friend us on Facebook today! **Keller Music Academy for the Low to Moderately Talented.** P.S. We even discount for the least talented kids!

◆

McDonald's a Very Bad Setting to Explain Slavery

Suburgatory, USA—A local mom is kicking herself for choosing McDonald's to explain slavery and its legacy to her six-year-old son. "The legacy of this stupid decision, well, I'm going to live with it 'til at least the seventh grade when Teddy finally actually understands slavery. That is, unless we are ripped apart in the giant race riot he causes before then," said Jan Maxwell.

Jan and Teddy were heading to lunch at the Boone Street McDonald's; Jan was listening to *Fresh Air* with Terry Gross on public radio. As part of Black History Month, Gross was interviewing an author about the history of the slave trade. "Terry Fucking Gross. Another white liberal moron just like me," Jan said, berating herself.

As they arrived at the McDonald's, Teddy and Jan ordered their food and sat down. It was then that Teddy asked his mom, "What's slavery?"

Jan: *Well, Tadpole [Teddy's nickname], this is hard. Slaves were people with darker skin who were forced to serve other people—lighter people like me and you. They had terrible jobs, doing the same boring or tiring thing over and over and over . . .*

Teddy processed this, looked at the entirely black or Hispanic staff of McDonald's sweating, stone-faced and slinging fries with lightning speed, and then looked at what was, on that day, the entirely white clientele, mostly moms and kids, eating contentedly.

Teddy: *You mean, like them?* [pointing to the counter] *They are slaves?*

Jan: *No, no, not at all, Tadpole! Slavery's over. They get paid. Slaves didn't get paid. They got food and a place to sleep, that's it.*

Teddy: *Oh, that's good. I'm sure these brown people get a lot of money now after all that slavery stuff.*

Jan: *Well. . . .*

As a mother, Jan knew that being honest about salaries at McDonald's might complicate matters immensely. But as a good liberal, "like Terry Fucking Gross," Jan made the regrettable mistake of being honest.

Jan: *Well, actually, I'd be lying to you if I said they do. They don't make much. Very little in fact. They make enough to just get by, but not much more than that. It's a hard life.*

Teddy: *Do they at least get to eat the food?*

Jan: *Um, no. They take their small amount of money from McDonald's and buy food, probably somewhere else, like we do, at the store.*

Teddy: *So slaves got paid in food and these brown people get a teeny bit of money and buy their own food?*

Jan: *Yes.*

Teddy: *Then what's the difference? They* are *slaves!*

Jan: *No sweetie, they're not. No one owns them.*

Teddy: *If McDonald's pays them their tiny money and but doesn't feed them, then doesn't McDonald's own them?*

Jan: *No . . . look, Teddy, they don't make much money but they aren't slaves. They have their families—slaves mostly didn't have their kids with them. Moms lost their babies.*

Teddy: *What about* those *moms?* [gesturing to the women working behind the counter] *I don't see any brown babies here. Where are their brown babies?*

Jan: *They put them in daycare—you know, the place to keep them so the workers can do their work for McDonald's.*

Teddy: *So McDonald's takes them away!*

Teddy started crying and said, "I don't want my Happy Meal if a brown mommy gets her brown baby taken from her!" And then, before Jan could grab him, he ran up to the counter and said, "I'm so sorry you are slaves and I'm a slave-maker! You shouldn't be slaves!"

Jan said, "Teddy, no!"

Then he told white people in line that they were "slave-makers," too.

Maxwell shudders even recalling it. "Basically I've turned my son into a little Malcolm X. A Malcolm X who still wets his bed."

Will she go to McDonald's again? "No. From now on we're getting served by mostly white people only. Teddy X better start liking Starbucks."

◆

Dog Fed Better than Scholarship Child, Says School Nurse

Suburgatory, USA—A concerned school nurse asked for a meeting with the mother of Tom Mason, a scholarship student at Bundy Academy, upon deciding that her dog is fed better than the student.

"A dog is a child, *my child*, and of course I feed Roxie only hormone-free grass-fed beef, real cheeses and yogurts, pureed vegetables, whole wheat pasta, brown rice, and flax seed," said Jenny Maurice, who added that on special nights he gets "prepared dinners," including one described this way on the menu at the high-end Delicious Ruff Doggie Bistro: "Ground Shoulder of Farm-Raised Beef served over Couscous and Oven-Roasted Leeks. Served with a sauté of Fresh Pan-Wilted Kale, Fresh Garbanzo Beans, Roasted Polenta, and Hint of Garlic. Then drizzled with High Oleic Kosher Olive Oil." Maurice said, "I know, I know, it sounds a tiny bit excessive, but it really keeps Roxie's coat shiny."

So with all her attention to Roxie's diet, "and my own," she added, Maurice was disturbed when she saw Tom's monthly diet diary, which is required of all the students. "You're damn right I requested a meeting with his mother!" said Maurice.

This reporter asked whether she also requested that the boy's father attend.

"Oh come on," she said, exasperated. "Father? What father? What planet are *you* on? Even if there was a father, and I doubt it, I wouldn't call him. They're pretty much all useless, no matter where they come from."

Maurice decided that Mason's mother wasn't going to be receptive after it took a week to set up the meeting. "Oh, because I'm a bad mother? Is that what she thinks?" said mother Terry Quillan. "You know, he is with his dad half the time but I'm guessing she didn't call *him* in for a meeting. Which took me a week to set up because we live twenty miles from school and I *work*. At Clucky's Chicken. They don't give you a ton of 'me-time' at Clucky's Chicken."

As Maurice and Quillan sat down together, Maurice placed a sheet down showing the new USDA "plate" with its nutritional recommendations. "Ms. Maurice, I'm fully aware of what's healthy and what's not," said Quillan.

"Well, not to overstep . . ." said Maurice hesitantly, "but Tom's diet diary had a lot of carbs and not much high-quality protein like, say, wild salmon, and no real 'rainbow' of fruits and vegetables. It looks mostly frozen or from cans and certainly not organic or locally sourced. Now since I care so much about this issue, I took it upon myself to talk with the folks at Whole Foods to put together a possible meal plan for you!"

The list included Pineapple-Chicken Kabobs with Quinoa, Fruit, and Hemp Seed Muesli, and Lebanese-Style Grass-Fed Ground Beef Kabobs.

"I thought the chicken and grass-fed ground beef would be more affordable for you. Things like wild sea scallops can really add up. I know firsthand!" said Maurice, hoping to be helpful.

Quillan looked at the list in enraged wonder. "This food would wipe out a week's worth of food stamps in two meals. Tell me, is my son doing poorly in school? Is he overweight? No, he is neither. He eats what I can afford and what he'll actually eat. And what he eats at his *father's house half of the time*. This meeting's *over.*"

As Quillan stormed out, Maurice lovingly fingered the frame on her desk showing Roxie's photo. "Oh Roxie. You are so lucky to have me."

◆

Discount Doula "A Really Bad Choice"

Suburgatory, USA—A couple admits that hiring a "discount doula" was a "really bad choice," making the delivery of their first child unforgettably awful. But their nightmare had an unexpectedly happy ending.

"Yes, looking back, trying to save money on a doula was a big mistake," said Alysia Verderese. "But I just thought that anyone who calls themselves a doula is probably a caring, thoughtful person. Anyone who even knows what a doula *is* is probably a caring, thoughtful person, right? "

"My mom never heard of doulas," said husband John.

"I rest my case."

The couple was hoping for as natural a birth as possible and thought a doula labor-and-delivery coach could help, especially because Alysia's mother was dead, and she would have had no women in the room with her. But with money tight, the Verdereses found a Craigslist ad that read "Doula For Less Moola." John seemed embarrassed upon being reminded of this. "Yeah, I guess a doula with a corny, rhyming name should have been a tip-off. And the University of Phoenix reference."

But Alysia appreciated the honesty of discount doula Maggie Brown and got a "warm vibe" from her ad:

I am offering my services at far less than the going rate, because I admit to being new to the delivery room. But I do have certification from the University of Phoenix and proven experience in very stressful human situations. I love meeting new people! And I look forward to making your birth experience an unforgettable one!

Alysia Verderese prided herself on taking chances on people. "I've always tried to help the little guy, and every doula has to have a first time, right?"

Once labor began, the couple arrived at the hospital and met Maggie Brown there. "Ummmm, I expected a kind-looking, natural older woman," said Alysia. "Translation: an old lady, no bra, with an ass-length gray braid," said John.

Instead, Maggie Brown "looked like Joan Jett. Only meaner," said John. "Or *The Girl with the Dragon Tattoo*," said Alysia. "I thought she was going to man-snap all of a sudden and rip John's face off."

But Alysia did notice that the tattoos, scary at first glance, were actually half the cast of *Fraggle Rock* all over both her arms. "I mean, how mean could she really be?" asked Alysia.

Brown came in with supplies, which Alysia in her doula daydreams imagined might be aromatic oils, candles, and washcloths in an earth-toned, organic fabric bag. Instead it was a plastic Walgreen's bag with Cheetos, Capri Suns, the latest issue of *US Magazine*, tampons—"I was out," explained Maggie—and a package of diapers. Alysia took the diapers and said, "Maggie, we're in a hospital. They have diapers here. Also, these are for eight-month-old babies."

"Oh, does that really matter?" said Maggie. She threw herself down in the chair and started reading her *US Magazine* and eating Cheetos. "You want some Cheetos?" she asked Alysia, who replied, "No, Maggie, I can't eat during labor."

"Oh! Sucks to be you!" said Maggie. "Must have missed learning that one at ITT Technical."

"Your ad said it was University of Phoenix," John said.

"What's the difference?" Maggie said.

"She got me there," John admitted.

When Alysia started contracting, Maggie stood up and silently watched her, staring directly at her face. "Wow, this looks like it really hurts. Hurts like a total motherfucker. You poor, poor lady."

The nurse came in to see if she wanted her epidural. "Oh no no, no epidural. I have my doula here with me—" Alysia smiled tentatively "—to help me get through it." The nurse gave Maggie a slow up-and-down look and said, "You look like Lisbeth Salander, the 'Girl With the Dragon Tattoo,'" "Oh my God, THANK YOU!" Maggie said, momentarily elated. "Wait, is the epidural the pain stuff? Dude, don't be crazy! You have to get it!"

Alysia: *Maggie, I told you I wanted a natural birth. Do you even know what a doula is?*

Maggie: *Well, the lady whose dog I walk—she's kind of rich like you—she had one and it sounded so, so, caring and thoughtful.*

Alysia: *Yes! See, John? Caring and thoughtful.* [John rolls his eyes.] *Exactly. But I'm not rich. I mean, maybe to you I am.*

Maggie: *Well, anyway, dude it's totes your body and for whatever reason you seem to want to suffer, and I really really don't like to watch people in pain or suffer! You wouldn't say 'no drugs' at the dentist's office getting something pulled out of your mouth, would you?* [She starts to tear up.]

Alysia: *Maggie, what did you mean in your ad when you said that you had 'proven experience in very stressful human situations'?*

Maggie: *Oh . . . well, I was in Iraq. One day our supply convoy got hit. I was OK, but, it was bad. So now I just want to do happy things like help babies and mommies and shit.*

John said, "Great, so now I had *no chance* of throwing her out of the room. First, she's Lisbeth Salander, weirdo punk doula, and now she's Lisbeth Salander, American fucking hero."

As Alysia's contractions got stronger and stronger, Maggie covered her face and kept repeating "I can't watch! I can't watch!"

Alysia, panting, said, "It's OK, Maggie, you'll be OK!"

When the Verdereses' son finally emerged, and Maggie saw the blood, John said, "I swear to God, she got the thousand-yard stare."

But then, once little Cory was cleaned up, Maggie slowly walked toward him and, like Alysia and John, looked utterly transformed. "Hi, little man! Hi, little man! I'd take such great care of you if I could just figure out what to do and get my act together a little bit and let this piercing heal up a little better, and I'm really good with dogs," she said, softly touching his fingers and toes and nose. "Do you guys maybe need a babysitter sometime?"

Reader, they hired her.

◆

Mommy War Combatants Embrace Mutually Assured Destruction

Suburgatory, USA—Combatants in the Mommy Wars have achieved a carefully calibrated detente, with each side amassing large stockpiles of vastly destructive Guilt, Pity, and Scorn bombs.

Both the stay-at-home moms and the working moms have absorbed the lessons of Mutually Assured Destruction, which helped keep the peace during the Cold War. That means the combatants make it clear the weaponry they possess, so that each side knows an attack by one would result in total annihilation of both.

Valerie Snow, accused war criminal and guerrilla leader of the stay-at-home moms (SAHMs), described her side's weaponry while cutting decorative radishes for the evening's PTO volunteer appreciation dinner. "If they so much as *hint* that we might have something better to do with our time than making decorative radishes, by God, they will live to regret it."

Snow describes the catastrophic impact that would result from deployment of their Guilt, Pity, and Scorn (GPS) bombs against the working moms.

"Well, our carefully engineered GPS bombs would unleash some devastating, shattering intelligence. They would inform the working moms each time their children said, 'Why can't *my* mommy volunteer all the time like you do?' (Which happens all the time, just sayin'.) They would disclose the intimate details the child shared with a stay-at-home mom because, where the hell is their own mother this time? Oh yeah, working, because of her pathetic priorities. They would catalog all the joys the working mothers had missed while on the job—the first soccer goal, first crush, weekday summer visits to the local pond. And they would throw in some anecdotes from empty nesters dying to have their kids back and wishing they had done things differently, like *be with their children.*

Amber Ostroff, who leads the working moms (WMs), betrayed no fear of the other side's lethal capacity. "Oh please, you think that's gonna scare us?" said Ostroff, speaking from the Dallas-Fort Worth airport where she was en route to a client meeting. "We are corporate lawyers and doctors and college professors. Remember college, ladies??? What was that even for again? Right, you got an Ivy League degree in making decorative radishes." Snow flinched upon hearing the statement and the radish crack, but maintained control.

The WMs' own GPS weapon, designed by a working mom engineer at a leading defense contractor, would strafe the SAHMs with the charge that they insult poor and working women by suggesting there's any "choice" in staying home for most women. It would inform them that they are weak role models and an "insult to every feminist who fought to get them in the workplace in the first place," said Ostroff. It would force stay-at-home moms to talk about "anything other than their kids." Says Ostroff, "Good luck with that one, ladies!"

Their GPS would also feature new research suggesting that overparenting is hurting, not helping kids, and statistics showing that stay-at-home moms who give up careers take an enormous financial risk if their husbands decide to divorce them and snap up a younger model. When that happens, says Ostroff, "The SAHMs turn from being parasites in their own home to parasites on the whole nation." It would also question whether they had remained sexually appealing to their husbands. "Ever see a working mom in a hideous pair of mom jeans? *No.* We have some self-respect."

With these equally fearsome weapons aimed at each other, both sides have been able to manage a very fragile peace. "While your leaders fight the public battle, we suggest that when our SAHMs see a WM, that they just be polite and ask one token 'How is work?' question, and try to leave it at that. If the WM starts droning on about how challenging her latest project is or bragging about a big raise, we'll advise the SAHM to just excuse herself and go back to collecting box tops."

"Agreed," says Amber Ostroff. "Keep it all on the surface, smile and nod, smile and nod, and as long as they don't start passive-aggressively guilting me about these stupid school events I've missed, we might all make it out of this alive."

◆

SHOUT OUT

Walk All Over Me, I Don't Care, but Don't Call Me a Perv

The Halden Street sidewalk, known to local police as the "Sidewalk Perv," was installed over an eight-month period two years ago.

Listen up, there's a reason this is called Shout Out, townspeople. I am the Halden Street Sidewalk, *not* the Sidewalk Perv. I might be a little rough around the edges and have a few chips and cracks. I am made of gravel and rock, after all, and yes I do come from that industrial park across town lines where only the trucks go and the Oxy addicts squat. Excuse me for not being classy enough for you, Halden Street.

Now I'm not saying I'm easy to like. I do hate a lot of you. I hate fat people pounding on me, but I hate those crazy joggers even more; scary bitches, faces all scrunched up in terror like they're being chased by the big bad old-age monster. Guess what? He's coming for you anyway! Also, I hate people in wheelchairs barreling over me all day long without a thought in the world. I hate snow and drunks who puke on me and those mouth-breathers who spit their gum on me, and most of all, of course, every damn dog on the street shitting in my face.

But what I like, I like a lot. And that's the ladies. Is that a crime? I like all types of ladies, except the fat ones and the crazy joggers. And, come summer time, pull up a chair, because I got the best view in town. Yeah, when I saw those pink french-tie hip hugger panties Cindy Kramer was wearing yesterday, yeah, you could say it made my day go a little faster. And if you ladies go all Lindsay Lohan and ditch the french-ties, the booty shorts, the boy leg briefs, g-string thong, or the classic high-waist bikini altogether, giving me a show of a lifetime, that's *my* fault? It seems like *you're* the Perv here, Miss Eileen Marple, not me.

But I want to make one thing absolutely clear. I do not *ever* look at an underage girl. Who do you think I am, Roman Polanski? When a young lady in a Catholic school uniform walks over me, I turn my eyes deep into the bowels of the earth, and trust me, what's down there is not pretty. I am no pedophile. I am a completely passive lover of women, not a menace. So stop walking all over me, curb your dogs somewhere else, and stop shitting on my good name.

◆

Mom Plans School Auction During Dreary Sex

Suburgatory, USA—A local mom who is a skilled multitasker used her once a week love-making session with her husband to plan her school's much-anticipated school auction.

It's hugely, massively important to the PTO's budget, thought Sheryl Winnick as her husband Dave ran his finger up her calf and asked, "Did you shave?" That was a typical signal to begin their lovemaking, along with the comment, "Hmmmm, you smell good," and a playful head nuzzle.

"Yes, I shaved," she said. This was his cue to perform mostly perfunctory oral sex on his wife. "Oh no, it's not fun at all but I so appreciate his effort. It's just a nice courtesy." *Now . . . I was thinking a good theme would be Arabian Nights,* she thought, as he continued attempting and failing to pleasure her.

Arabian Nights . . . would that sound too . . . Muslim? Well, screw those bigots, that's so ignorant. Anyway, maybe the PTO moms could wear harem outfits. "That's it, give it to me, honey . . ." This was her way of telling Dave it was time to perform her own perfunctory and generally substandard oral sex on her husband. "Yeah it's lame," he admits. "She's bad at it, and tonight I know she is planning the auction while blowing me, but you know, it's so important to her. I'll take what I can get."

At this point, says Dave, it was "go time," and he entered Sheryl from the side, which was typically a two-minute prelude to the finale: climax for him and perhaps her, occasionally, through the tried-and-true missionary position. *We'll get the VFW Hall and have a preview the night before, thought Sheryl. We can do a spa package, haircut certificates from Snippety Crickets, what else? A grown-ups Wii party . . . that actually did great last year . . . ski house weekend. . .* "OH YES!"

At that point, Dave finished and Sheryl gave out a hearty, but secretly forced, gasp. Dave was satisfied despite the fact that Sheryl's mind was clearly elsewhere, and pretended to have an orgasm. "You can see how devoted she is to the school and the kids. Marrying her was the best thing I ever did."

"Honey, should we watch the *Daily Show* now?"

"Sure!" Sheryl said, snuggling up to her husband. *I wonder if Jon Stewart would ever sign a book for us to auction off at Arabian Nights—he's always defending teachers. Hmmmm, now how would I get in touch with him?*

◆

Guidance Counselor Feared, Loathed as World's Sole Remaining Hyperpower

Suburgatory, USA—Area guidance counselor Mavis Goodstone has been declared the world's undisputed hyperpower by some of our region's most prominent residents, who were discussing Goodstone's massive, destabilizing power while attending the World Economic Forum in Davos, Switzerland.

Goodstone is renowned locally as the high school guidance counselor with the "golden touch" in terms of college admissions. But few parents have been able to decipher her motivations or her delphic comments, and many are left enraged by the capricious and arbitrary ways that she decides who to help and who to spurn.

"That frigid bitch used her power to keep my kid out of Harvard, and I *teach there*," said historian of empires past and present, Denis Ferguson. "Since then, Goodstone has amassed unparalleled military and economic might. A unipolar world is a dangerous world, and Goodstone is a very dangerous and, I should add, very unpleasant woman."

Hedge fund manager Gareth Faber agreed. "Yeah, you know people hated Bush. But at least *that* decider was pretty personable. *This* decider won't even make eye contact." Faber, whose son is applying to Brown, still has no idea if his child is on Goodstone's anointed list.

"Goodstone's currency is just murdering the dollar and the Euro and you know, my wife Jenny just texted me to say Golden Goblin [Goodstone's nickname] appeared a little aloof this morning when she went in to discuss Tristan's applications, and now she is fuh-*reaking* out. Total disregard for human rights."

Some predicted, and hoped, that Goodstone's overweening power and hubris would lead to her eventual downfall as a hyperpower. "She's pushing the envelope. Her preemptive strike on Syria, her runaway deficit spending on arming herself, and her tactical blunders—snubbing Anna Wintour's daughter?! Who snubs Anna Wintour? Oh I know. Mavis Fucking Goodstone. In her JC Penney pantsuits," said foreign policy expert Hassein Makaria. "All these bold but shortsighted moves could signal the end of a long, and, as history will prove, ugly reign. Gareth . . . um . . . did Jenny mention how Goblin acted toward [Makaria's wife] Valerie? Her appointment was right before Jenny's."

Faber became agitated. "Where did she even go to college? Have you heard her do assembly at that open house? Can she even speak proper English? How did that woman get to be the global hegemon? I just don't get it."

The participants at Davos tried to get their underlings to negotiate with Goodstone while in attendance at the World Economic Forum but their diplomatic entreaties were harshly rebuffed.

"I don't know what I'm supposed to do. Write a column for the *Times* that just says, 'Bitch, Call Me Back'? Like that would do it, I'm sure she doesn't read the *Times*. She's *USA Today* all the way," said *New York Times* oracle Thomas Friedman.

Friedman went on, "Folks, pull up a chair and listen. Humiliation is the most underrated geopolitical force, and if I don't get a callback soon, she's catching hell, and I'm calling for sanctions. That piano-legged shrew. She will be her own undoing."

◆

Dr. Drama

"When life hands you a problem, let's make it more interesting!"

Dear Dr. Drama:
I think my husband, I'll call him "Tom," is flirting with other women on Facebook. I should say, I **know** he is flirting with other women on Facebook. It is making me really crazy! What should I do?
—Face-Freaked in Suburgatory

Dear Face-Freaked:

So let me guess. The pictures "Tom" has up on Facebook are the best pictures ever taken of him to the point that you barely recognize him? And for some reason you don't seem to be in any of them? And aside from the flirting, does Tom post updates like "Didn't ever think I could bench-press that much!" or "Margaritas chilling in the fridge, marinated steak on the grill, relaxing on the deck. LIFE IS GOOD." Am I right?

Well, you could ask Tom to stop flirting, sit down like grown-ups, and ask, "What's missing here that you need to take to Facebook for stimulation?" and boring boring blah blah. But I have a much more satisfying idea.

You're going to reveal the real Tom on Facebook. You surely have photos lying around of Tom with his crack showing or his flabby stomach sagging or stuffing his cake-hole with Funyuns, say. Simply post them, preferably at times he's not on Facebook, and tag him. He won't be around to untag and there he is, in all his real Tom disgustingness, for all his little pathetic nubile groupies to see. You could also pepper in Wall comments like "Honey, the bank keeps calling about the foreclosure, can you *call them back?" or "Are your hemorrhoids feeling better? I'm so sorry they kept you up last night!"*

With Facebook customization, you can even hide them from everyone you know! (Thanks, Zuckerberg!) The only ones who'll see it are strangers, and, of course, those cunts makin' time with the fake, attractive Tom. That way, you can get back to having the true Tom, the repulsive slob you love more than anything in the world, all to yourself.

◆

Dad Invents Label for Unruly Child

Suburgatory, USA—Frustrated with his failed attempts to get his unruly child labeled, a local dad has taken matters into his own hands, promoting his own made-up label as a genuine disability to other parents and his child's teachers.

"Oh, yeah, Kilkenny has FG-NOS: Franticocious Gravidarum—Not Otherwise Specified. It combines rare academic talent with a frenetic, sometimes uncontrolled pace. Kilkenny is compelled by his expansive mind to explore boundaries, so that explains the inappropriate touching incident. It's something, you know, the schools just have trouble keeping up with. But we're going to change that," said Kilkenny's dad, Jerry Lipton.

When the school district intervention team was asked about FG-NOS, it had no knowledge of the disorder. Lipton was undeterred when presented with this information.

"FG-NOS is cutting edge. Fifteen years ago, who had ever heard of Asperger's? People who were troubled geniuses were considered retarded, warehoused. I refuse to give up on my seriously disabled child, and neither will this school district, not while I'm paying taxes here."

Kilkenny's teacher, who chose to remain anonymous, was nonplussed by Lipton's assertions. "I don't know what the hell he is talking about with that FG-NOS or whatever that was he was spitting at me at the teacher conference. All I know is Kilkenny is just a seven-year-old jerk, pure and simple. He won't listen. He throws stuff. He can't spell his own name. He groped little Madison! The other kids hate him. And I can't say I blame them. 'Rare academic talent?' Where the fuck did he get that from? Not from my teacher conference, I can tell you that. I can't wait to tell Principal Harris. She's going to laugh her *ass* off that he talked to you about his 'disorder.'"

Lipton asserts that FG-NOS will soon be part of the roster of well-established developmental maladies that require classroom assistance and government-supported occupational therapy. He expects it will be added to the next Diagnostic and Statistical Manual of Mental Disorders, or DSM.

"You know I bet forty years from now we'll look back and realize that some of the giants of yesteryear—David Hasselhoff, Michele Bachmann, all the Kardashians—they had undiagnosed FG-NOS and were misunderstood as the quirky child geniuses that they were. And my Kilkenny will be able to speak out as one of the first to say 'I had it, I'm hugely successful now, and you can make it out the other side, too.'"

Indian Child Taunted as "New Jew" at Middle School

Suburgatory, USA—The District Attorney is investigating a possible hate crime at the Lexington Middle School, after an Indian child reported being taunted as a "New Jew" by several classmates.

The student, Nikhil Chaudry, thirteen, said that four children, over the span of approximately one month, referred to him as the "New Jew" after Chaudry captured the high score in the regional televised teen trivia show, *Answers Please*.

Chaudry's family arrived from India four years ago and quickly developed the successful Currying Flavor chain of restaurants. They have been seeking, and gaining, political influence with large donations to politicians on both sides of the aisle.

The Chaudry child is described by his teachers variously as "a superstar," "a relentless worker," and "a joy to have in the classroom." One said, "if only I had twenty more like him."

They said Chaudry's academic success and the family's emerging prominence has apparently engendered resentment among the other children.

The Chaudry child gave a statement to reporters. "One kid said I was the 'New Jew.' He said we just hoard all our money. Another kid chanted 'New Jew, New Jew' and said 'You people want to take over the world. You took our jobs over there and now you want them here and I'm going to end up going to Green Valley Community College.' Another one said 'We don't need you making us look bad every day to Mrs. Kelley. Don't you have a Wii? And where's your iPhone? What do you do after school? Sample SATs?' Someone else said, 'You people can make all the money you want but my dad said you are still going to smell like curry no matter what [expletive] Ivy League school you get into.'"

Chaudry added, "I didn't actually think it was that bad. I thought they were going to call me a terrorist or something. I didn't even know what they meant by 'New Jew.' It was my mom and dad who got really mad, after I told them."

Parents of two of the accused bullies spoke on condition of anonymity.

"Nikhil doesn't play any sports. It's just school, school, school, school. Now how are our kids supposed to compete academically against that? I think activities should be weighted along with academics. I mean, does our country really need all these single-minded brainiacs? Is that the message we want to give the kids, that soccer is meaningless and that the teamwork they learn in lacrosse doesn't matter? That's not my America."

Another visibly angry parent said this: "By the way, why do you think his parents are pushing this case? To raise his profile even further? Of course that's why. It's good free advertising for Currying Flavor, like they need any more, and it'll make Nikhil stand out even more on those college applications."

No matter the outcome of the case, Nikhil Chaudry believes he'll have the last laugh. "They can call me 'New Jew' all they want. All I care about is getting into MIT or Cal Tech and making tons of cash. And in twenty years they'll be pumping gas into my Escalade, at one of the gas stations my cousin Naresh owns. And I'll be married to Miranda Cosgrove. I'll be bigger than Zuckerberg."

SHOUT OUT

In Fifteen Years, Awkward Girl, You'll Be Totally Hot

Nathan Brodie is a novelist who lives on Mareau Street.

As a college professor I do quite a bit of work at home, as my desk points out the window of the red house with yellow shutters. Each day I see the young, fresh teenagers trundling past me from the high school. In a strange way I feel as if I have gotten to know them, in my fantasies, in an utterly nonsexual and nonthreatening way.

So know this, if you ever read this, Awkward Teen Girl with the red windbreaker and funky retro purple glasses: I am not stalking you. (You hear that too, Awkward Teen Girl's father? No need to come a-knocking on this door! Nothing but pure intentions on my part!) This is merely a paternal word of advice. Awkward Teen Girl, you'll be totally hot in fifteen years.

Now, I know, you don't believe it. The popular boys surely have no use for you, and you've already gotten used to that. But what you're realizing *now* is that even the barely cute geeky ones, like I used to be, don't like you either! Well, they don't know what they'll be missing in fifteen years. The Pretty, Not-Awkward Girls have figured out their look at age fifteen and it's all downhill from there. Trust me, I know all too well. Having no originality, because it is not required of the Pretty, Not-Awkward Girls, they rest on their aesthetic laurels and cling to that one trashy look that worked so well for them in high school. Well, by thirty, that ain't looking so great anymore.

You, on the other hand, Awkward Teen Girl, are already struggling to distinguish yourself from the Pretty, Not-Awkward Girl and this is making you stronger! By twenty-five you'll have given up your adorably funky glasses for something more professionally appropriate for your challenging and exciting career. You'll be getting your hair, nails, and toes done and feel great inside and out. Look to Tina Fey—and see your bright, Not Awkward, Totally Hot future.

Believe me I wish I could shake those boys who spurn you and say, "Don't make the mistake I made!" But that's how life works, as you probably know already, because precocious wisdom is surely one of your signature gifts. Sadly, that's just one of those talents that alienates or threatens teenage boys, but is utterly charming to a forty-year-old man. So I just want to assure you that in fifteen years, I'll probably still be here, rooting for you in a nonsexual way. Now you know where I live, if you want to wave, please do! And it's true what the gays say, sweetie, it really does get better!

◆

Santa Asks Child for New Liver for Christmas

Suburgatory, USA—Santa Claus, the giver of joy and delight to children the world over, today asked a four-year-old local boy to wish for a new liver for Santa, and gave the back-story on his cirrhosis diagnosis, along with other maladies.

"Hi, Santa!" said Nick Gardner, as he leaped onto Santa's lap at the town's high-end Northway Mall. Gardner lives with his parents in the affluent Westgate neighborhood.

Santa: *Why, hello boy. Merry Christmas! What's the name. Oh, Nick? Hey, don't bounce too much, boy, got some stones I'm passin'. Wha-chu want for Christmas, little man?*

Nick: *Um um um I want the Power Rangers Operation Overdrive Mega Mission Helmet . . . and the . . . and the . . .*

Santa: *You know what I want, Nick? I want to kick this infernal cirrhosis. Let me tell you a little story, Nick. Back in the '80s, my woman, Mrs. Claus, had a little problem with a very dangerous game, let's just call it "smack."*

Nick: *Smack, smack, smack!*

Santa: *My lady and I, we were travelin' 'round this great big country—you know, when we're not at the North Pole—parking our RV at whatever KOA we could find, takin' in whatever life brought our way. KOA is Campgrounds of America in case you don't know. . . .*

Nick: *I've never been camping! I swim in the hot time at the Club! You know what else I want?*

Santa: *. . . and Mrs. Claus couldn't stop playin' that smack game. And there was a whole passel of people at the campgrounds who played that game, too. And then Santa started playin' that game, too. Again and again and again.*

Nick: *That musta been fun, Santa!*

Santa: *Well, I'm not gonna lie, Nick, Santa loved the game and so did Santa's lady. Those were some crazy times for your ole Santa. Matter a fact, I think about playin' that game all the dang time. But now I got a little something called cirrhosis. And now somethin' real important inside Santa—Santa's liver—well, it's shot.*

Nick: *Oh gross! I hate liver! Mommy tried to give me that because she said, she said, she said it's got a lotta good iron in it! It makes me grow important like Daddy to make big money! It grows my brain! [Nick put both hands to his head.]*

Santa: *Well, Nick, you wouldn't like my liver at all. It's all scarred up and spent and hard like the coal we give bad little boys, not like you, the bad ones I'm talking 'bout. Santa's got his own list you know, a list for a newfangled liver, all fresh and shiny and red and tied up with a bow. But, well, it's in God's hands now.*

Nick: *But aren't you, aren't you, like God, Santa? Could you call him on your Santa phone?*

Santa: *Ho! Ho! Ho! That'd be a real kick in Santa's big red pants if he could! Santa would get a brand new liver for Christmas and maybe even get rid of that sweet blood, too. I shouldn't make it sound all that bad, Nick. That darn cirrhosis is why my tummy is so puffed up and that's how I got to be Santa here at the mall. And this year, Santa needed work. Santa needed it real real bad.*

Nick: *You're a silly Santa, Santa! See you next year!*

Santa: *Well if you are a very good little boy, and wish for Santa to get that new liver he was tellin' you about, you just might see me next year and I'll have lots more silly stories 'bout me and Mrs. Claus to tell you.*

Nick: *Bye Santa! Merry Christmas!*

And with that, Nick and his mom, who was on her iPhone during the whole discussion, left for last-minute shopping at Bloomingdale's.

◆

Dad Forcibly Removed from Mall Massage Chair

Suburgatory, USA—An unemployed, reluctant stay-at-home dad has become an unwelcome regular at the Brookstone within the struggling Atrium Mall. Yesterday he was forcibly removed from the Ultimate Robotic Human Touch Massage Chair.

Ian Brown was unrepentant. "I don't know what the big deal is. Don't you think seeing someone in ecstasy sitting in that chair for a little while is good advertising for Brookstone?" Brookstone associates offer a starkly different portrayal. They say Brown has been frequenting this particular chair for months, several times a week, and stays for at least forty-five minutes each time.

"First of all, we've been trying to cut back on people parking there, so we put a sign on it saying 'Please ask an associate before you use the chair.' He just takes the sign and throws it on the floor."

Another associate says Brown has a technique for ignoring the store employees. "He just sits down and closes his eyes immediately. But I can see him do these tiny squints. He's watching us. And he's obviously awake—he just parks his kid's stroller in front of him and lets her scream. And when the auto program stops at the end, he just picks up the remote and hits it again. With his eyes still closed."

The supervisor is worried about the physical condition of the chair and also the safety of the child. "Sometimes to shut the kid up he drags her onto the chair with him and all that machinery, God, I don't even want to think about what could happen to that little body. And then there is the 'groove.'"

The "groove," as he calls it, is the indentation Brown is leaving in the chair. The supervisor said, "If corporate comes in here, and sees that groove on a three-grand chair, I'm going to get my ass handed to me."

This is what led to yesterday's forcible removal. First they tapped Brown, and then said, "Sir, we know you are awake and your child is crying." When he was roused, Brown grew combative, screaming, "Don't call me sir, motherfucker! I'm just an out-of-work dad who needs a little break. You college flunky dipshits get a break. What about me?"

Sources say after some tense discussions, he came to an agreement with security that he would take his child to Build-a-Bear, and then leave the mall immediately.

◆

Contractor Distractors

Bored out of your mind in your marriage? Look over at your mate and think, "I wish she'd buy some new clothes" or "I wish he would pluck that disgusting ear hair?" Always wanted that sundeck you never knew how to pull off? Well, at **Contractor Distractors,** we build your dream deck and rekindle that flame at the same time!

With a maddeningly complex design plan, multiple changes, and constant no-shows you'll forget all about those freakish bunions. With the budget running over and the total tally mounting, you'll be sitting amid exposed two-by-fours and dangling electrical fixtures for months on end. You'll be attending cocktail parties where the "nightmare" is all you'll be talking about. You'll have one common enemy and it won't be each other: It will be us. That's a guarantee. And by the time we're done, which won't be soon, your marriage will be as sunny as a July afternoon of Mojitos on your new sundeck. So when home improvement meets marital malaise, think **Contractor Distractors!** We are currently offering a midlife crisis special: The kitchen of your dreams with two full years of hassle . . . and hugs.

◆

Pedophile Quietly Mourned as Amazing Coach

Suburgatory, USA—A convicted pedophile is being quietly mourned by local dads as an "amazing" and "outstanding" girls' varsity soccer coach.

"That disgusting pervert. It took months to put that psycho away," said parent Kevin Mainer about Tom Miller, who was charged with statutory rape against several minor girls in February and convicted last week.

"But," added Mainer, a bit sheepishly, ". . . well . . . I mean, uhh, now we're shit outta luck if we think we'll kick Benchley School's ass ever again."

Other parents agreed. Said Paul Hofstetter: "Oh yeah, if it was my daughter? He'd be fucking dead right now. I'd have his ball sack run up the flagpole. I gotta give it to him, though, anyone who saw that upset he pulled off last year against those amazons from Holston, I mean, whoever takes over is gonna have big shoes to fill, that's all I have to say."

The men went on to debate the gravity of Miller's crime. "Come on, just a few decades ago, this wouldn't have even been a crime. Those girls were marrying-age back then. What if we were in Utah?" said Nick Natola.

One mom joined the men, speculating about whether the crimes might be considered consensual. "Yeah, I know one of their parents; the girl says she's 'totally in love' with the pervert, so we know she wanted it. And I heard the other charges were trumped up. It was just backrubs with their shirts off. Believe me, I remember being that age. I knew exactly what I was doing."

Several dads wondered if some special accommodations could be made. Mainer had this to say: "Couldn't they just give Coach Miller one of those ankle bracelets? I mean, for this to happen mid-season? Did you see the looks on the girls' faces?"

One dad, Donald McPherson, a professor of cultural and gender studies at Carlson University, termed the arrest a "classically American witch hunt, a puritanical sex panic that you would never see in Europe. . . . And good God, what a coach."

As a Level 2 sex offender, Miller will now have to register with local police if he returns to the community. When confronted with that possibility, no parent was ready to accept Miller back as a neighbor. But as a coach, they feel like they could work around it.

"You know, the parents could take turns monitoring him every minute he's with the girls," said Natola. "Let's face it. The guy's a douche. But he's got a gift. One of those we'll-never-see-the-likes-of-him-again-once-in-a-generation kind of gift. To throw that all away, jeez, I don't know. It just doesn't seem right."

◆

Dad Loves Carving Ducks, Parenthood

Suburgatory, USA—A local dad says parenthood "is the best thing that ever happened to him," as he made his way to his basement shop to spend the evening carving ducks.

"Hi, kids!" Steve Anthony patted five-year-old Parker and three-year-old David as they watched the PBS show *Arthur.*

Once in Anthony's shop, this reporter saw twenty or so carved ducks in various states of completion.

Anthony said this about his role as a dad. "I never thought that I could have this much love, this much patience for my kids."

He fired up his Dremel Multi-Max power drill, which, Anthony says, is when the kids usually come down to say hello. Sitting at his table with the Dremel motor whirring and his kids standing silently at the door, Anthony yelled over the sound of the power tool: "I love that I'm able to share this beloved hobby with my children and that they'll be able to share it with their children."

The kids then returned to *Curious George* and turned up the volume due to the noise of the Dremel. "Mallards, buffleheads, egrets, you name it. . . ." Anthony said, as his wife arrived in the shop with his dinner, which he takes nightly during carving. "The kids know all the ducks' names by now, what kind of feathers they have, what makes them distinct from one another. I'm so lucky to have them and the kids."

Several hours later, Anthony had completed a mallard. "The boys are just such a dream. Every moment with them is just a new way to see the world, through their eyes." The boys arrived at the shop to say goodnight to their father. "Goodnight, boys! I love you!"

Parker said, "I love you, too, Dad." David said, "Bufflehead Bufflehead Bufflehead!"

"Aren't they just little miracles?" Anthony said, smoothing his hand over several of his finished ducks.

◆

SHOUT OUT

Let's Do that Key Party *Right* the Next Time

David Dowd is a polyamorous swinger who lives on Larrabie Street, the house with the purple door.

To say I was disappointed about the conduct at and disintegration of my long anticipated key party last Saturday night would be a colossal understatement. This is not a "hobby" for me, or a one-time lark. So I take to the Shout Out in hopes of making sure the next key party is done right.

Some ground rules:

First, just because I am overweight, a bit hairy, and missing that one tooth (which I'm getting replaced, by the way), you cannot put the key you chose back in the bowl hoping to draw someone else. Number one, you really hurt my dignity. Number two, you denied yourself a banging the likes of which would erase every sexual experience you've ever had. Your loss. But if you don't want to lose out again, take my words seriously.

Second, my parties are not for bored moms who watch *Cougar Town* or *Desperate Housewives* and want to do something naughty. Or say they did something naughty at the PTO meeting. Because when they actually get to my home, even when dressed like the tackiest forty-year-old prostitutes I've ever seen, they are not willing to get down to action at all. This violates the spirit of swinging. I don't care that you're hot. If you're not going to let me or another of your neighbors give it to you, and give it to you hard, you could be Angelina Fucking Jolie herself and I'd still kick you out of my house.

Third, it's a party for *swingers*, not exhibitionists. To that couple who just came in to fuck in front of us, we say, take your sick pathology elsewhere! You need to hand your partner over to a complete stranger for sex, and she will do the same with you. That's swinging with *integrity*.

Fourth, we *don't* have daycare for your kids. Please, get a goddamn babysitter. There's only so long we can stick kids upstairs to watch *Fanboy and Chum Chum*. Now this party was a big bust, but most parties are not and they are quite loud. You want your kids to hear that, dirty bastards?

Now, I'm left with shattered expectations and more Fritos and leftover seven-layer dip than I would ever eat in my life. So next time, please, come committed, come with condoms, or don't come at all.

◆

Purchased Breast Milk
Tainted by McDonald's

Suburgatory, USA—Breast-feeding activists are up in arms after one working mother purchased breast milk later found to be contaminated by McDonald's.

The mother, Tinsley Maher, corporate lawyer for Proskauer Rose, purchased what she called "premium" milk at four dollars per ounce, after her own milk supply dried up. "Good God, I wasn't going to give Maeve formula. I work eighty hours a week. I couldn't pump. So I found some on ThanksfortheMammaries.com. And then this happens."

Maher felt like her daughter "just wasn't her unique, singular self when I was reading a bedtime story to her one night on Skype. Maeve's essence just wasn't there." She suspected the breast milk might be to blame and had the Board of Health test the samples in her freezer. The Board subsequently found traces of the Angus Beef Third Pounder, Sausage Biscuit, and, most troubling to Maher, the McRib. "McRib. Nanny Elvie has been giving my baby girl liquid McRib. In a bottle."

Maher is particularly troubled because the source of the milk came from within the well-known local breast-feeding collective and progressive social group called the Titty Tribe.

"I mean, if this came from a disadvantaged person, someone for whom McDonald's is part of their culture, what their people do, well, then I would understand. Even if maybe she was a poor single mother or something, and was desperate for money and sold her milk. I understand that deep socioeconomic disparities can drive people to do sickening, crazy things, like eat McDonald's," Maher said. She noted that

she was a sociology major at Smith and had read *Nickel &
Dimed* by Barbara Ehrenreich on the flight to a client meeting. "Proskauer Rose has a great program every year where
we paint festive murals [in poor urban neighborhoods] and
clean up their filthy playgrounds," Maher said.

"But this was 'premium milk'! The mom is part of the
Titty Tribe, for Chrissake! She eats at McDonald's, and then
sells her revolting, corporate, pesticide and growth hormone–
filled milk to *me?*" Authorities say they would prosecute if
they could, but there are no laws on the books that pertain to
McDonald's-tainted breast milk. "There will be soon enough,"
said Maher. "I didn't go to Harvard Law School for nothing."

The mother who sold the milk refused to give her
name. She has weaned her own child but is still lactating and
thought she was, in her words, "paying it forward by selling my precious mothers' milk." She says in her defense that
she does not normally eat at McDonald's, but that pumping
breast milk makes her "lose her mind" and "eat like an animal." "I only went through the drive-thru a few times," she
said. "I never thought it would show up in a test. I just hope
I didn't do Maeve any lasting damage. I'll never do it again."

◆

you in that situation in the first place: your insatiable, truly unquenchable appetite for a little drama. And at **Sober Sully's,** we provide the drama you crave *without* the alcohol and resulting DUIs, marital heartbreak, and end-stage liver failure.

Starting at 8:00 p.m. each night, our "bad behavior" is professionally facilitated by actors who will turn **Sober Sully's** into that veritable crazy train of dysfunction you loved so much. Loved *too* much! Whether it's Rolling Thunder Night, Toxic Gays Night, or Saturday Sluttytown, **Sober Sully's** will engineer, say, the unexpected biker brawl or the sloppy kiss with the age-inappropriate stranger or the bathroom line bitch-fight. Hair will fly and we can guarantee there will be a nipple slip or two. But what happens in **Sober Sully's** *stays* in **Sober Sully's** and absolutely no alcohol is involved in any way. No law enforcement needed! Other than maybe a few actors who *look* like the police, because we know how much you aging suburbanite drunks love and *miss* the rush of a good bust.

Sober Sully's—"One day at a time" just got *a lot* more interesting. Join us, and bring your sponsor, too!

◆

Mom of Eight Amazingly Taut, Except for Vagina

Suburgatory, USA—An energetic mother of eight is a local legend at her fitness club for her "amazingly taut" body, but she has revealed exclusively to this reporter that her vagina is not included in this characterization.

"Oh no no, are you kidding? God has allowed me to birth eight beautiful babies the way He intended! I have to wear a cup to keep that thing from flip-flapping around at the gym!"

Laurie Bishop is well-known in the community for being pregnant for much of the last fourteen years, during which she has maintained her lithe body until the very end of the last trimester. She is also known as an active member of the Junior League, a resident of the exclusive Westgate community, and an avid churchgoer who abstains from alcohol.

"We've been so blessed, so blessed. God sent Sofia, Fernando and Paco, Sylvia, and Oksana to us," Bishop said, referring to the household staff. "And Beeta. Ugh I always forget Beeta. Well, whatever, they are my superstars. I could never manage Team Bishop without them!"

Does her husband mind the slackness of her vagina? "My husband? You mean that useless piece of skin attached to my credit card? Ha! No, I shouldn't say that. Bryan is the leader of our family and our relationship comes before everything, including the kids, like the Bible says it should blah blah blah. I just let him do his business and it may take a little longer but hey I can always go over the kids' day plans in my head so it's no big deal at all, really! An hour and he's done. And then, if God thinks it's right, we get another precious baby."

Bishop could afford vaginal reconstructive surgery, and indeed has received enhancements to her face and breasts. But she has no interest in vaginoplasty because she views her gaping birth canal as her "gift to God," and also because her husband doesn't complain. "Complain? Bryan? You're confusing him with a guy who has balls."

While at the pharmacy, Bishop said, "And anyway, this is what my Lord God Jesus Christ put me on Earth for. Oh yes, I'm picking up for Bishop? Yes "Klon-o-pin." The stuff that knocks you out?" With that, Bishop muttered "fucking morons" before brightening. "No, I don't have any questions, thanks. God loves my vagina for what it's done, its joyous bounty. Would I like the flubbering and the occasional whistle to stop? Of course I would. I wouldn't be human if I didn't. But other than that, I wouldn't change a thing."

◆

Four-Year-Old Gets Perez Hilton as "Manny"

Suburgatory, USA—An old-school couple unwittingly hired celebrity blogger Perez Hilton as a "manny" for their four-year-old son, who in turn schooled them all in his special brand of queeny humor.

"Well, we know him as *Mario*. I just thought Mario had a lot of energy and fun hair and I enjoyed his whimsical outfits," said mother Susan Topping Huntington, who was born into one of the area's oldest and most prominent families, and married into another. Mario Lavandeira is Perez Hilton's real name.

"He was like a performer I'd seen who did gorgeous origami at the holiday benefit for the kids at the library. My salon guy, Jeffrey, really recommended him. And I loved that he was a Mario who spoke such perfect English," said Huntington, unaware that Hilton's main job is reveling in Hollywood gossip on his heavily trafficked website, and until relatively recently, drawing cocaine and semen drawings across the faces of targeted celebrities.

"He did seem a bit, well, a bit of a dandy. But he is a rather tall man, and these days aren't like the old days. We really have, how should I put this delicately, quite a lot of financial interests that make it crucial for Robert to have a man guard him rather than the traditional Scottish nannies we grew up with."

Investment banker Peter Huntington soon noticed some odd behavior from Robert. "He kept talking about 'Perez' and 'Perezers.' One day he ran into the great room and asked me who was more—what was the word he used?— 'fierce,' I think. 'Who was more fierce, Miz Dita Von Teese or Miz Kylie Minogue?'" Both parents assumed that these were teachers or specialists at the exclusive preschool Robert attends. They are actually a burlesque star and an aging pop singer, respectively, both lionized as divas by Hilton.

It was Peter Huntington who finally discovered Hilton's true identity while attending a benefit for at-risk youth. Featured was Hilton's anti-bullying testimonial for "It Gets Better." He also learned that Hilton had recently toned down his site and had stopped drawing those apparent cocaine and semen scribblings.

When confronted by the Huntingtons, Hilton told them, "You caught me! Took you hella long to figure it out!" And when asked why he decided to become a manny, Hilton said it was part of his reinvention from viciously catty to more mainstream. "I got tired of drawing cum and coke on people's faces. No more calling Jennifer Aniston 'Maniston.' I was tired of being the cattiest 'Queen of all Media' and wanted something real, authentic. And Robert's a great kid. He totally brought the ferocity on some of La Lohan's captions. He loves RiRi [Rihanna] and Selenita [Selena Gomez] as much as I do. And I just got a cameo on *Glee!* I realized pretty fast, dahlings, this bitch can't quit."

◆

From the Offices of "Dr." Victor Brown

Do you want a psychotherapist who will maintain appropriate boundaries, YAWN? Or do you want your sessions to feature the crackling sexual tension you might have seen between Paul and Laura in the HBO series *In Treatment?* If you're like most bored, mildly depressed housewives, I'm guessing it's the latter.

And I, "Dr." Victor Brown will take your "erotic transference" and run with it! My practices have run me afoul of the American Psychological Association, and thus I am no longer a certified therapist, nor can I travel beyond the town line without notifying authorities. But I can assure you that you will leave our sessions tingling and exhilarated. Now, I may be a little more Abe Vigoda than Gabriel Byrne, but I can still daddy you up with the best of them. Call the doc, and let this "Paul" take care of all your needs, "Laura." One hour will never fly by so fast.

◆

Child with "Mullet" Pressured to Leave School

Suburgatory, USA—A six-year-old child has been pressured to leave his private school because his "mullet" hair style has been deemed "disruptive" and "disturbing" by school officials.

Officials at Hamilton Knoll Academy refused to comment on the matter, but several parents, who all requested anonymity, described the controversy. "No one here has one of those trashy mullets! My kid kept coming home and asking me about it. 'Mommy, [name withheld to protect the child] has this really short hair in the front and long in back! What is that, Mommy?' I don't want my child to have to know what a mullet is."

This reporter met with several concerned mothers at a local Stitch-n-Bitch meet-up on Central Street. "Look, I just got done explaining what Diwali is to my Eamon. It was so confusing for him. And for me, frankly. Now I have to explain what a mullet is? I seriously didn't think anyone still had those!"

Another parent tried to explain to her daughter that this child came from "another culture." The girl asked, "What culture, Mom? Is he Native American?" The parent remarked, "What was I supposed to say? The kid's white trash? My daughter knows culture. She's been to Venice!"

The attendants of the Stitch-n-Bitch gathering were asked to describe the parents of the child in question, who were unavailable for interview. In the words of one mom: "You know, it's really weird. They can afford the tuition, but they have a dumpy car with a public radio sticker, and so for a while I thought, 'Oh, they must be lesbians! That's why the kid has a mullet!' But they weren't lesbians. I saw the dad at Open House."

The mothers were nearly unanimous in agreeing that it would have been much easier if the parents had, in fact, been lesbians, as this culture has already been well examined in the typical kindergarten curriculum.

Another mother who attended that open house said: "Yeah, I was thinking before I saw him, 'Maybe he's a famous ex-hockey player? And has a family history of hockey hair mullets?' But he was a total schlub."

One mother disputed the notion that the family was white trash. "No way. Not with that public radio sticker. I heard they don't even have cable. And their last name sounds Jewish. Jews aren't white trash. But a Jew with a mullet? I mean, I'm at a complete loss with that one. Could they be hipsters? Is it an ironic mullet?"

She agreed that regardless the mysterious cultural background of the parents, the child's mullet was an unwelcome distraction for her child. "McDermott could not stop staring at it. He's got ADHD. It's hard enough for him to keep it together in the classroom. I'm just glad the head of the lower school agreed to do something about it."

◆

Dorothy, we will guarantee that one of our fantastic stylists *can be that friend.*

Haven't you always wanted to wow those drab straight friends with lines like this: "Well, my fabulous stylist friend Dave was hooked on meth for *years*—he calls it 'Tina'—he said you could have sex for days on end! But after a lot of rehab, and the love of a good boyfriend, he's OK now . . ." or "My gay friend Scott, he's so fabulous, he just saw my hair and said 'girlfriend, you call that shaggy animal *hair?!* That looks like overgrown pubes on your head! Let's fix that bad boy for you!'"

Your fabulous gay stylist friend will also joke about how hot your husband is, but actually he's not kidding about that part. Every six weeks, you'll get your one-hour dose of fab, *and* the hottest hair design available within fifty miles. Why do we know it will be the hottest design? Because your Friend is gay! And very, very gay, we might add.

So call us now and get your own fabulous friend at **Friend of Dorothy.**

*Note: **Friend of Dorothy** does not discriminate, but we don't employ lesbian stylists, not because of their orientation, but because the modern straight woman simply doesn't consider them catty or bitchy enough. This bias does not reflect the views of **Friend of Dorothy Salon.** We know plenty of bitchy lesbians.

◆

Child Can't Convince Mom She's Beautiful Inside and Out

Suburgatory, USA—A local mom insists she is "fat, hairy, and hideous," despite the protestations of her son, who tells her she is beautiful "just the way she is."

"Mommy, why are you crying?" said six-year-old Brian Gardner to his mother, Judi Gardner, who was hand-tweezing some stray lip hairs after a wax appointment earlier in the day. "I'm just getting rid of the hair, honey, no big deal. It's just . . . just gross!"

Brian was troubled by this. "But I like you a little fuzzy, Mommy! Like here!" Brian touched his mother's arm. "*Ugh!* See, even you noticed my freak arms. Mrs. Sasquatch. I have to do something about that. Maybe laser."

"Sabers? Like *Star Wars?!* Mommy, that sounds scary," said Brian.

"No honey, *LASER.* It's not scary. It just burns all the hair off with a scorchy light and you just have to wear special glasses and make sure to never, ever look at the light. Not scary at all!" Gardner said, as she boarded her home elliptical machine and Brian settled into the chair and snack tray he sets up during her lengthy sessions.

"But Mommy, I thought you said that God loves all of us just the way we are!" said Brian. "Yeah right, God's never seen this giant flat ass of mine," Judi muttered.

"What, Mommy?" asked Brian.

"Nothing honey, you're right. God does love us just the way we are. But other people aren't nice like God is," she said breathlessly, as she increased the resistance on the elliptical. "You know when you see those other mommies at school, when they're guest reader or volunteering at the library, how good they look?"

"Mommies are beautiful, all mommies, but you're the most beautifullest in the whole world," said Brian.

"Well, I will be, after I get something called dermabrasion," Judi said, panting.

"What's that, Mommy?" Brian said.

"Oh, it's where they sand your yucky face off." Brian looked terrified. "No, Mommy! Your face is my most favorite face!"

"Honey, it's OK, I'll still have my face. It will just be as soft as a baby's bottom."

Brian started to cry. "I don't want your face to look like a butt! That's where poop comes from." Judi tried calming him down but continued on the elliptical, saying, in short bursts, "Sweetie . . . I meant that . . . it will be super soft . . . you'll love it."

Brian got up from his chair and tried to play with his mother's stomach while she was exercising.

"Soft like your fluffy tummy, Mommy? It's so warm and squidqy." Judi paused the elliptical, got off, and appeared triumphant.

"You see? Out of the mouths of babes. I *knew* I was fat. Kids don't lie to you about that stuff—they tell it just like it is." She ruffled Brian's hair. "I'm so glad I have him around to keep me honest. Brian, who's the best little man in the world? You are! Someday I know you'll meet a wonderful, beautiful girl who'll love you exactly like you are, just like your Mommy does."

Mom Literally Dragged
Back to Suburbs

Suburgatory, USA—After two days of traipsing around Manhattan reliving her carefree single-girl days, an area mother had to be literally dragged back to the suburbs.

"Ma'am. It's time," said New York City police officer Peter Clark. "*Noooo!!!!!!! NOOOOOOO!!!* Get your hands off me!" wailed a belligerent Trink Giroux as Officer Clark heaved her into the back of the car. "Watch your head getting into the cruiser, ma'am! Did you just bite me?"

Giroux was reported missing by her husband one night ago. She joins hundreds of mothers in recent months who have fled their homes and responsibilities, leaving their husbands utterly unprepared to handle their children's hygiene, homework, and food requirements.

"Fucking God. That was like right out of *The Sopranos* when they took Adriana for a 'drive' in the country," said Officer Clark, shaking his head in contempt and looking for teeth marks in his hand. "She was fighting it hard, all right, real hard."

Giroux was picked up while trying to pose as a twenty-something hipster at a Lower East Side club, which she *thought* was Tonic. But Tonic has closed since she lived there. A new club is in its place, and after noting her dowdy attire, dated haircut, and weary, medicated expression, the actual twenty-something hipster manning the door immediately notified police that there was an escaped mom inside the establishment. "What are you saying to me?" she kept asking the young man. "What? I don't get what you're saying." It appeared that he was speaking mostly in the unaffected style of Mumblecore movies, a trend Giroux has utterly missed because of parenthood. She found the hipster's speech patterns incomprehensible, which enraged her further.

From the back of the police cruiser, Giroux tried to explain leaving her family and home to Officer Clark. "I just wanted to turn back the clock, just for a day or two. No whining kids, no clueless husband, no 'accident reports' from the preschool. *NO* goddamned *OLIVE GARDEN. NO PLAYDATES.*"

"Do you realize what you've done, Mrs. Giroux? You left your little kids in the hands of their father. The school said one of your kids came in with a single mitten and another with no scarf. No juice boxes either. Your husband thought Fruit-by-the-Foot was real fruit. Their field trip forms, remember those? No, you don't, do you? And you don't care. You're disgusting. You are disgusting to me."

"You're right, you're right, I am disgusting," Giroux said, weeping as they made the inevitable slog back to town through the commuter traffic. "I just wanted to go back. But you can't go back, can you? Not even for a visit."

Back-stories

Okay, I didn't need to be *literally* dragged back to the suburbs, like "escaped" mom "Trink Giroux," but let's just say that a lot of the material in this book was based on personal experience. I wish I could dish even more dirt I've heard over the years, but I have to be careful in giving you the back-stories, at the advice of counsel. (I've always wanted to say that! It sounds like I've arrived!) So if this stuff sounds very much like "me me, more about me!" the reason is simple: I don't have to worry about suing myself.

The "escaped mom" piece and the one that led the book, "Atheist Mom So Lonely She Accepts Christ," were among the very first I wrote back in 2007—when I was still praying to Brooke Shields, the patron saint of deeply depressed mommies. I was then and still am an atheist. Sort of like, "God? Come again? Oh yeah, THAT dude!" But loneliness is a powerful motivator, and it was a mom friend, Liz, who first suggested going to a Baptist church playgroup/"parenting classes" by saying, "I'm a Jew from Jersey, and I *love it!*" At first, this idea seemed—hmm, what's the formal term—'ass-stupid'? Still, I began going, and sure enough, this battle-scarred ex-Catholic got an unexpected religious education. The Christ I knew from childhood seemed like He was saying, "Look what a scary mess I am because of you, sinner! Guilty now? Good!" But at this Church, their Christ looked serene, as if He were fresh from yoga class.

I was constantly stepping in shit, yet they always politely looked away. I asked one of the ladies, "Oh, what's Ryan going to be for Halloween?" And she said, haltingly, "Well, we don't celebrate Halloween." I looked over at my son, who was wearing a snaggle-toothed pagan pumpkin, and my friend Naoko's son, sporting a merry white skeleton, and I thought, "Great, we just paraded our boys around their church in Satan-shirts."

I was bowled over by their hospitality to me. But I still felt like a fraud, hiding my lack of faith and boundless social liberalism, and I wondered if at, say, a gay rights rally or pro-choice rally, would my new friends be on the other side of the line? Did I care?

Well, I do care very much, as a long-standing fag hag, about gay rights. In "Lesbian Hamsters 'Just Grew Apart'" I am definitely the annoying "Flora" who foists my homophilia on my child. We have a really old game of Life (free from the town dump) with the classic blue and pink pegs, and I actually did tell my son that "a blue peg should be able to marry a blue peg if they love each other." Now my son asks his friends when playing, "Do you want to marry a blue peg or pink peg?"

You might notice, ahem, a little anger in places over breast-feeding. When I told an (ex) pediatrician that breastfeeding wasn't working for me, while looking disheveled and ready to careen off a bridge, she looked at me as if I had served her a turd on a plate. I wanted to say, "You know, a near-suicidal mom is quite the problem, too, lady, and breast-feeding is making it worse." Just a note, ex-ped: My kid has no allergies, so here's a heartfelt "fuck you" to you.

I have spoken to at least a dozen women about the guilting they've gotten over breast-feeding, and for a while I got sucked into a real online breast-feeding collective, which I called the Titty Tribe in "Purchased Breast Milk Tainted by McDonald's." I found it fascinating how obsessed they seemed to be with breasts—their own and other women's.

They seemed to be mostly highly-educated, third-wave feminists. I was flabbergasted that a few seemed willing to take even untested bodily fluids from perfect strangers rather than bottle-feed, as I mention in "Wolf Blitzer: Live from the Lactation Room."

Closely allied to the breast-feeding guilters are the natural birthing guilters, the target of my ad for "C-Secrets," a business that will give you a believably "natural" birth story to throw off finger-waggers. This is in tribute to friends Colleen, Kate, and all my many, many other C-section moms who've been told the only "true" way to have a baby is through your vagina. Sure, C-section rates do seem excessive. (Call that the Ricki Lake *Business of Being Born* concession.) But that doesn't mean women should demean one another about such a private experience that the vast majority probably had little choice in making.

You might notice Wal-Mart gets a starring role a few times in the book. I'm intrigued by Wal-Mart's role in affluent suburbia as a class divider. Few friends will admit to going there. "Terry Gotlieb" in "Woman Shops at Walmart to Feel 'Pretty, Thin'" was actually based on a woman who one day described Wal-Mart shoppers as if they were sub-human. Wal-Mart is the single most diverse place I visit in suburbia. Chuck E. Cheese comes in second.

I also get my cheap on at the town dump, described in "Join My Weirdo Junior League!"—which is almost entirely true, except for Dumpster-diving and the very end, when my friend Laura notices I'm wearing her discarded shirt. That actually did happen, but I got the shirt at her school thrift store, where I've gotten literally $1,200 worth of clothes in one bag for, oh, thirty bucks.

Laura is the unexpectedly sane leader in "PTO Stunner: New President 'Not a Power-Mad Psycho.'" Now, the PTO leaders at my son's school have been fantastic—nothing at all like the evil PTO terrorist Emily "Bin Fahdin." But that supermarket ambush by a crazed PTO honcho actually happened to a friend in another corner of Suburgatory. This piece was also inspired by working parent friends who feel shut out of PTO. I see a lot of lip service given to the idea of "Can't we all just get along, mommies?" But the fact is, I see a whole lot of judgin' going on everywhere. That's what inspired "Mommy War Combatants Embrace Mutually Assured Destruction." I so hate it when women tear each other apart.

Oh, who am I kidding? I *love* it!

Really, though, I wished I could have worked more into the book for working moms, but I'm a stay-at-home mom. It's what I know, it's pretty much *who* I know, and many pieces reflect my efforts to combat whiny white mommy malaise. Besides the church, I did become an IKEA regular and a mall semi-regular who bought nothing but took massage chair breaks, not unlike the "Dad Forcibly Removed from Mall Massage Chair." And I am the pathetically eager, unstoppable Facebook queen lambasted in "Mom Crushed to Learn that Facebook Isn't Job." If you can believe it, not one but *two* apparently single Pakistani mariners did friend me through the Jewish Maritime Historical Society. But they are not learning how marvelous the US is: All they're learning about American women, from me at least, is that we dress and speak like whores.

You might notice race comes up quite a lot, and race is certainly whispered about in the very white towns I've lived in. The playground encounter described in "'Funny Racist Lady' Enchants Prominent Black Townsman" actually happened to a friend. She is in no way racist, and I doubt the famous black athlete would be "enchanted" if she was. But my friend did think the other park-goers were being racist for subtly pointing at them. And he did invite her home for take-out, which is when she figured out he was a superstar and apparently a very nice one at that.

Other moments I can cop to include an acquaintance referring to Indians as the "New Jews" because of their fierce determination to succeed. It had that strain of admiration plus disgust I see in anti-Semitism. The Ice Cream Man really is universally hated by my parent-friends, no matter his religion or color. But I did indeed meet someone who talked about one of them—a "brown" man of indeterminate ethnicity—as if he was a gypsy at best or a terrorist at worst, saying, "Just who ARE these people?"

One of the fun things about writing this book was getting back the very insightful copyeditor notes from the whip-smart Imee Curiel. In a couple spots, she said, "Come on, this is just far-fetched." But in the grand cliche of fact being stranger than fiction, these instances were actually real. There is indeed a high-end car in town with a bumper sticker that says HAD ENOUGH?, which is what inspired "Mercedes-Driving Dad Dreams of Easier Life for His Children." It was a different fancy make of car I couldn't place. (Being Super Crazy Mega Cheap, I don't know a thing about new cars; my own cars are old enough to start cramming for their PSATs.)

I wanted to tailgate this guy, to ask, "Had enough of what?" Inherited wealth? Profound luck? Because I can say without hesitation that the vast majority of people I've met who live in affluent suburbia got here by growing up affluent, marrying someone affluent, or getting themselves advanced degrees through hard work but also because they won the IQ lottery—better known as luck. That's how I got here: luck. So, yes, rich dad apparently fed up with your enviable life, I've had quite enough. Enough of you and other rich people complaining endlessly about their taxes.

One person who endlessly complains to me is a delightfully inappropriate mom friend determined to snag an invite to a supposed swinger party held each year on Halloween. I really did think that key parties were suburban folklore, but I've since been convinced that, while surely a teeny-tiny subculture, they actually do exist. I have no doubt that if we did go, we would be the moms who are all talk and no walk that swinger "David Dowd" complains about in his Shout Out. Though I would be all over his seven-layer dip.

I do love my trashy food, and at some point, obsessive "foodie culture" began to both annoy and alarm me. It alarmed me to think that the healthiest food seemed to be becoming the sole province of the affluent, which is what inspired "Dog Fed Better than Scholarship Child, Says School Nurse." And like the character "EatMyShit" in "Waitress Wages Anti-Foodie Jihad on Chowhound," I became irked by constant Facebook pictures of everyone's spectacular, one-of-a-kind dinners. My own response to this is on Facebook was a "Moms Against Food Porn" picture series I did of really gross crap food sitting around my kitchen.

And there's quite a lot in here about women aging and loathing their own bodies. I go through phases when I become obsessed with one topic, and for a while it was that photo-collage "Faces of Meth" described in "Woman with Eating Disorder Considers Meth." I showed it to everyone I knew, and no fewer than three mom friends looked at those ghoulish faces, paused, and then said, essentially, "Wow, meth really makes you lose a lot of weight, huh?" The fact is, I thought the same thing and hated myself for even thinking that.

And I leave you with one more self-loathing incident that I didn't explain fully in "Child Can't Convince Mom She's Beautiful Inside and Out," because I thought no one would believe it. I did go through a midlife crisis a few years ago, the cheapness was very briefly tossed aside, and I actually bought laser hair removal—bikini line—on an impulse buy. It came with a special bonus: micro-dermabrasion! The day I went to redeem my "bonus," I brought my son. (*Too cheap for baby-sitting, but not for lasering? Hypocrite!*) When I got there, they said, "So sorry, we have you in for lasering your bikini line, and you'll be charged if you cancel." So, yes, dear reader, my son sat in the corner, oblivious, wearing oversized protective glasses that kept slipping off his face, while his mommy sat on a table, legs spread, getting her bush lasered off. At least, I thought he was oblivious, until I heard him say, "Mommy, why are your pants on the floor?"

Acknowledgments

I had this fear that some of my work might seem, at times, woman-hating, so I'm happy to see how many actual women I have to thank here.

To my sisters Joellen, and especially on this project, Terry (plus Benno and Ron), who pushed me to get a backbone.

To the amazing Laura Yorke and Carol Mann at the Carol Mann Agency in New York, to Steve Fisher at APA in Los Angeles, and to attorney Eric Rayman. And thank you to Willow Bay, for connecting me to Laura Yorke. Laura saw just a few writing samples in 2009 and said, "You must write something."

Laura placed this book with another superstar, Lara Asher. Besides being a terrific, turbo-charged editor, Lara got the material instantly and is just a lovely, spunky force. And thanks to project editor extraordinaire Meredith Dias for her expert execution.

To beloved college friend, architect David Tabenken. David named this book, and I am only sad his wonderful mom, Helen, along with my own Mommy, aren't here to see David's title appear on national television. To my Aunt Nancy, Uncle Matt and J. Spellman, among the few people left who knew and loved my Mommy and Daddy.

To my favorite Reuters anchor, Jen Rogers, who fought hard alongside my sister in making this project happen. I consider Jen a sister in everything but blood. The same goes for my dearest college friends—Rachel Laiserin, Lisa Epstein Jay, Tina Hohn Schissel, Geri Clark, and Ashley Gravelle Morse—as well as CNN's finest, Rachel

Brown (who brought me sisters-in-crime Peg Rettino and Joanna Joplin) and all-around producer/ball-buster Amber Briscoe. And to my honorary brothers: scary-smart journalist Chris Nolter, my first friend at CNN and someone I still treasure all these years later, and the brilliant Dr. Scott Schissel.

To bosses and boss-friend hybrids who accepted my considerable idiosyncrasies over the years: Steve Rosenbaum/Pam Yoder, Kathleen Campion, Kathy O'Hearn, David Bohrman, Jen Zeidman Bloch and Gene Bloch, the late Jeff Gralnick, Andy Breslau, Warren Kozak, Terry Baker, the irrepressible star-producer Kara Kasarjian, and especially Jenny Harris, a force of nature I was blessed to sit next to and learn from for years. Jenny makes that Holly Hunter character in *Broadcast News* look like a slacker.

To Hillary St. Pierre of Baldie's Blog, whose courage against cancer leaves me slack-jawed daily, and to her son Xander, who's even braver than she is.

To Arianna Huffington, who, at a dark moment confidence-wise, responded to an email seeking help in, oh, forty-five minutes? Thank you.

To some of the real parents of Suburgatory, the friends I'm lucky to have in town: Adam, Alex, Alexandra, Carl, Dan, Doug, Glenn, Glynis, Jen, Jeremy, Jim, Julie, Laura, Liz and Liz, Mark, Michele and Michele, Molly, Nancy, Naoko, Sandra, Sarah and my book club ladies, Suzanne, Valerie, and Yuki. I left out last names, in case I get run out of the state and some of you get run out with me.

Finally, the two groups people who made Suburgatory bearable besides my actual family and helped save me from postpartum depression: my Facebook family (those I know

IRL, and those I don't). Wish I could name you all. You deserve your own sitcom. I'm working on it.

And, a diaspora of comrades who have fed me ideas and friendship and I needed a lot of both for this book: Adam, Alda/Bo, Alex, Alexandra, Alicia, Allison, Amanda, Ami, Amy, Andre, Andrea, Angela/Paul, Anne, Annemarie, Antonella, Antonetta, Bruce, Caitlin, Caleb, Cheryl, Chris, Christine, my "Church Ladies," Claire, Clint, Colby, Colleen, Dan, Dana, Daniel, Dave, Debbie/Ed, Derek/Manon, Diane, Dianne, Eddie, Elaine, Elizabeth/Kati, Ellen/Tom, Eric, Erin, Evelyn, Evelyn/Andy, F & E, Fitz, Flip/Tom, Frankie, Fred, George, Gretchen, Gudveig, Harold, Hasmeena, Iain, Ildi, Inger, Jackie, Jagger, all the Jennifers, Jess/Dan, Jessica/John, Jill, Jim/Geoff, Jodi, Johanna, Jonathan, JTL, Judi, Judy, Julia, Julie, Karen, Kate, Katey, Kelli, Kellie/Jens, Kerry, KimChi, Kirsten, Kirstin, Kitty, Laura, Leanne, Leslie, Leyea, Lindsey, Lisa, Liz, Lobo, Luis, Lynne, Marc, Marcia, Marcy, Marina, Mary Anne, Melissa, Merideth, Merlynda, Michelle, Nancy, Nicole, Pat, Penelope, Peter, Rebekka, Rev, Ripu, Rob, Robin, Roo, Robin/Lee, Roo, Russell, Ruth, Sally, Sarah, Sarav, Scott, Shane, Sharon, Sherman, Steve/Kyle, Sue, Susan, Susswein, Suzanne, Tanya, Tarun, Theresa, the Thibodeau and Morlock cousins, Tina, Toby, Tod, Todd, Tom, Tommy, Tony, Trader Guy, Tricia, Vanessa, Varman/Sarwat, and Wendy. Love to all!

About the Author

Linda Erin Keenan spent seven years as a CNN senior producer/head writer for top anchors including Anderson Cooper, Aaron Brown, Willow Bay, Stuart Varney, and Lou Dobbs during 9/11, the Afghanistan and Iraq Wars, the Dot Com rise and fall, several key national elections, and the New York City Blackout. Before that, she was at Bloomberg TV. It was 9/11 that pushed her to re-evaluate her 24-7 lifestyle, eventually trading it all in for baby and suburbia. Her first-person essays have appeared in the *Boston Globe Magazine* and the *Huffington Post*. She invites readers, especially the craziest ones with lots of problems, to friend her on Facebook.